GW01217688

Lysander Pil

Lysander Pilot

Secret Operations with 161 Squadron

by

James Atterby McCairns

TANGMERE MILITARY AVIATION MUSEUM

Copyright © 2016
by the Trustees of the Tangmere Military Aviation Museum Trust
Company Limited. All rights reserved. No part of this publication
may be reproduced by any means, electronic or otherwise, without
the written permission of the copyright proprietor.

A catalogue record for this book is available on request from the
British Library

ISBN 978-0-9935407-0-7

Published by
TANGMERE MILITARY AVIATION MUSEUM
Tangmere, nr Chichester
West Sussex PO20 2ES

Edited, designed, and digitally typeset by Reginald Byron,
Tangmere Military Aviation Museum

Printed and bound by Lollipop Print, Chichester PO19 8PN

Preface

I left school in the summer of 1965 and, after a gloriously long holiday, on 3rd October signed up as a cadet pilot in the Royal Air Force, subconsciously following in my father's footsteps. After successfully completing all the training that due to the political situation at the time was somewhat prolonged, I eventually became the youngest, albeit briefly, operational Phantom pilot in the Service. That was in 1971. Three years later with my first tour under my belt I was 26 years old and feeling quite pleased with myself.

To put that firmly into perspective, at the same age my father had already experienced everything written in this book and more besides, but, whereas I went on to have a rewarding career in aviation, Mac had only three more years to live; he died in a flying accident in June 1948. In that time, however, he managed to write his memoirs which, having been transcribed from his very hard-to-read handwriting, are reproduced here.

I never knew my father; I was only three months old when he died. My mother told me about some of his exploits but not all, and I, with all the arrogance of youth, accepted the situation and did not press her. I knew, for example, that he had been shot down over France and been made a PoW in Germany but I did not know how and where. I knew that he had made a daring escape and a successful "home run", but I knew little about the journey and nothing about being number sixteen on the Comet line. Of course I knew that he had become a pick-up pilot with 161 Squadron but most of the detail had eluded me. There was much to learn.

It was not until 1978 when Hugh Verity, having borrowed my father's unpublished memoirs, produced his excellent book *We Landed by Moonlight* that some of the clouds began to lift, and gradually over the intervening years further information came to light. More recently, through my serendipitous association with the warm and talented staff at the Tangmere Military Aviation Museum, the sun started to shine through. This book is the result.

In September 2015 my wife and I decided to visit Bad Sulza in Thuringia, the site of Stalag IX-C where he was imprisoned. There is a memorial and some of the buildings remain, overlooked by the old castle on the hill above the valley. We tried to imagine it in the depths of winter and how it must have been to crawl through the snow attempting to escape. We then drove to the railway station in Apolda and stood in the ticket hall among all the ghosts. I imagined how my father must have felt as he bought his ticket, the first of many on his journey to freedom.

Some days later we were in Bletterans in the Jura region of France where there is another memorial, this time to the Resistance and SOE pilots. The inscription reads like a Who's Who of 161 and 138 Squadrons. Subsequently, once back in England, we revisited Mac's grave in Retford Cemetery just to tell him what we'd done. May he continue to rest in peace.

I am not the author of this book, therefore I cannot dedicate it to anyone. However, had my father still been alive I know exactly what his dedication would have said: "To my Mother". So there you are, Dad, I've done it for you.

Finally, I would like to thank Reginald Byron, who put this book together from start to finish; David Baron, Dudley Hooley, and David Coxon for their friendship; and all the staff at the Tangmere Museum for keeping my father's memory alive. I shall be forever grateful.

Christopher James McCairns

Chapter 1

On Sunday, January 27th, 1946, a handful of people gathered in the Place des Invalides, Paris. There they watched the British Ambassador, then Mr Duff Cooper, hand over to the French Air Minister an operational Lysander aircraft. Few people in Britain or France knew of the simple ceremony. Fewer still understood its significance. But for those of us who were present it meant the end of an adventure and the fulfilment of a bond. The Lysander had been the service bus for the cloak and dagger racket. On the nights of the full moon these fragile-looking unarmed Lizzies used to fly staidly across German-occupied France, dodging night-fighters and manoeuvring round flak. Our landing grounds were rough meadows, lit by a trio of hand torches. Our cargo, out and return, was a load, usually heavy, of secret agents.

Now, with the public acknowledgement of its job, I could feel pride, in company with my colleagues, in saying "I was a Lizzie boy". For years during the war when we said that to friends we were greeted with upturned noses. Our Lysander unit was so carefully camouflaged and guarded that not even in the RAF did one person in 10,000 know of its existence and true functions. Lysanders were associated with the lowest of aerial occupations: target-towing, or at best, air-sea rescue. Certainly nobody thought of us as operational. To cover our tracks, and because our parent station was a Halifax aerodrome, we would refer to ourselves as "the kings of the four-engined bomber". Once I remember in a pub in Chichester shooting that line to a Belgian friend of mine, a man with whom I crossed the Pyrenees when we escaped from France together. I can still remember the scornful look of contempt on his face as one day on an aerodrome he saw me climbing into the Lysander.

The little crowd in the Place des Invalides was moving away.

I came out of my reverie and began to follow. Then a man touched me on the arm. He was a Frenchman. What we had called in the old days an "operator", one of the men who had found the landing fields for us and arranged our primitive flare-paths. The operator put his hand in his pocket and held out a big square of silk. "Here is your scarf, Mac" he said. I had been given that scarf at the end of 1942. I had put my Lysander down on a field near Compiègne in northern France, and before I took off I was presented with this handsome and fashionable piece of silk, a souvenir of Cannes Regatta. Like many flyers I had my super-stitions and this scarf became for me an invaluable mascot. In spite of repeated offers from girls, I refused to part with it, and I wore it every time I was on an operational flight.

Then one night in the summer of 1943 I was putting down a load of passengers in France when it went with the wind. After some experience of Lysander night flying, I had made it a habit to wind my left-hand window right down and, just before landing, stick out my left hand and wipe some of the oil from the wind-screen to provide better visibility.

This time the slipstream caused in the cockpit must have loosened my scarf, for just as I was about to touch down I felt the grasping hands of the wind tear the scarf from my throat. For an instant I forgot the business of landing. Letting go the throttle, I made a desperate effort to clutch the vanishing scarf. In my excitement I forgot to hold off, and the next thing I knew was that the aircraft hit the ground, bounced, and was airborne again. After that I did manage to neglect the scarf and was able to concentrate on the landing.

As soon as everything was under control I searched the cockpit, but there was no sign of the scarf. Slowly I taxied back to the little crowd waiting by the first torchlight, surveying as I did so every inch of the ground. Still no sign of it. I beckoned to the French chief operator in charge of the improvised landing strip, and tried to make him understand the importance of my lost mascot. He promised faithfully to try and find it and return it to me. I flew my passengers back in a gloomy state of mind.

But I still did not give up hope. The head of our group in London was an old friend of mine, and he even had a telegram sent to the operator, urging him to find the McCairns mascot. But nothing more was heard of it until the day of that grand reunion in Paris, when the operator came up and held it out to me. "Here is your scarf, Mac" he said. "The farmer who owned the field found it, and kept it until after the war without saying a word." The return of my scarf ended for me an adventure which had begun almost exactly four years before. It was in Brussels early in 1942 that I first heard of the Lysander unit. That may sound strange, but a lot of strange things happened to me in 1942.

Six months before the war I had enlisted as a volunteer pilot in the RAFVR, and in 1941 was a sergeant pilot flying a Spitfire with 616 Squadron of Wing Commander Douglas Bader's famous Tangmere Wing. On July 8th, 1941, I was told to report next morning to my station commander for an interview about my commission. A few hours later I was shot down, wounded and captured.

My first escape attempt was a failure. But on January 22nd, 1942, with a Belgian friend Lucien Charlier as chief plotter and guide, I got away from Stalag IX-C. On the first day we covered 250 miles by rail. On the second I became separated from my companion, but late that night I dropped off a slow-moving train into a snow-covered embankment somewhere near St Vith on the Belgian frontier. Where I was, or how far I had to go for safety, I hadn't the slightest idea. Physically weak, but quite optimistic in spirit, I trudged along the railway track. Then it happened. The blizzard started. It was the famous blizzard of January '42 — a storm which in the next three days was to paralyse all traffic in eastern Belgium and the frontier district. And it had to begin that night. For a time I managed to battle against it, with the snow blinding my eyes and stinging my face. I couldn't bear the way it whistled around my ears so I took off my white silk scarf and tried to make a decent headdress of it, putting it under my cap and round my eyes with it tied under my chin and flowing out to the rear.

Gradually I lost all powers of concentration. Mad ideas and nightmares went flitting across my brain. The blackness was terrifying — mile after mile of open waste. I pictured myself as the conqueror of these wild elements. I was the actor in a thousand and one impossible scenes, always battling against tremendous odds and invariably fighting through. For hours I must have lost all traces of sanity and became a primitive savage. But at length I could take no more and, seeing a house by the railway bank, the first I had seen for miles, I climbed up to examine it and, in a frenzy, started pulling at the doors. They were all locked and the sudden bark of a dog pulled me back to reality. I fled back into the blizzard.

Now I had neither reasoning nor strength. Every tenth step or so I would stumble and go sprawling between the rails only to pick myself up, babble incoherently and start running until I fell again onto the frozen ground. Try as I can, I am unable to remember the full story of that night. Only one or two major details still stand out. How far I managed to go in this manner I had no idea, but suddenly a huge shadow crossed my path and as I looked up I found I was under a railway bridge and that another track crossed my own approximately at right angles. How grateful I was for the protection of that bridge, for although the wind whistled through it, it did keep off the blinding snow and this gave me a chance to breathe and open my eyes. For perhaps half an hour I sat huddled in its shelter, trying desperately to focus my thoughts and decide which railway to follow. Gradually a little glimmer of sense came back, but only a glimmer.

With frozen hands I fished for my primitive compass, with the idea of locating west. There like a fool I stood, right in the middle of a railway track, with another crossing overhead, attempting to stabilise an inch-long bit of magnetised iron on a cotton thread 10 inches long which was swayed in all directions by the wind. When it did settle down I was mad enough to believe that it gave a magnetic north — completely oblivious of the effect of an iron bridge all round me. I, who had swung so many compasses in aircraft and corrected for deviation! Little wonder that there was 90 degrees error, which in my numbed state I overlooked. I continued along the railway line which led me north instead of west. Looking back, I can only credit it to the guiding hand from Heaven which had now so completely taken over my routeing. By 3 am I was utterly exhausted. Gone were all thoughts of the frontier and escape. Shelter was the prime consideration. I knew if I had to stay in the snow any longer I would surely go mad and die.

Suddenly out of the storm appeared light — apparently a very strong lamp and almost on the railway. I was convinced it was an aerodrome beacon. I tried to remember what I knew of German beacons. I was sure they were red, like this one. The idea of it being a signal on the railway I dismissed, for it was close to the ground and in no way resembled the many signals I had already passed. Once again I panicked as I recalled the placing of Hun airfields near railways. Thank Heaven I had been warned by this light and had not blundered into captivity. Obviously I could go no further, for whether the field lay to the left or right I couldn't tell, I turned and began my retreat. This was terrible — hope had gone because now it was manifestly impossible to cross the frontier tonight. All that added up to another 24 hours in this snow. Could I endure it?

Sobbing and babbling away to myself, praying desperately for shelter, I went back along the line until I caught sight of a tool shed I had spurned an hour before. I fought through the snow until I gained its protection. It was about 4 feet high, roughly 6 feet by 6 feet with one side exposed. In it were a couple of ploughs and agricultural implements, besides a few boxes which stood out of the drifted snow inside. I managed to drag one of the boxes into a corner and, sitting huddled on it, spent the remainder of my second night.

Writing this some three years after, I have no recollection of that evening save that it was sleepless and endured only by spasms of hugging myself whilst between sobs I called perpetually for divine assistance. Of concerted effort or scheming for the morrow there was none. Strangely enough in the snowstorms of late January 1945, I recaptured some of the same emotions, the same crazy ideas and nightmares but on this latter occasion it was only after momentary exposure. How those nights in 1942 were endured I simply cannot imagine.

From 4 am until 8 am on my third morning I froze in that shack, and then, as dawn appeared I washed in the snow, rearranged my silk scarf to a normal position, combed my hair and then struck off across the fields to where I thought there was a road. Sure enough there was a minor road, so as I struck it I once again turned and went west in the direction of the supposed aerodrome. After no more than a mile, I came across the cause of last night's frustration. It was a level crossing. The gates were still closed to the railway and although the snowfall had stopped and visibility had increased, the red warning light was still burning. That was my famous beacon which had forced me to abandon activities. What a fool I felt — one night wasted!

Along the road a small signpost announced that Weismes was the next village. Unfortunately that didn't convey a message, but at least I had hopes of finding my position when in the village. I plodded on very slowly. Only when people came in sight did I try to quicken my gait and sing out a hearty "Heil Hitler".

Towards 10.30 the village appeared, and almost the first building was the railway station, looking incredibly bleak and deserted. I walked up to the door and entered. Only a couple of other people were present, and to my delight there hanging up was an inch-to-mile map of the area. Sure enough, there was Weismes, just some 7 kms from Malmédy, the point at which Lucien and I had originally intended to cross. What could be better? Next, to cover up my presence in the station, I gazed intently at the railway timetable and saw that a train was due to leave for Malmédy in about 15 minutes' time.

My warped and by now over-confident mind whispered, "You have already done 400 kms over German railways, surely you can do the last seven. Come on, travel in comfort: it is cold, you are tired and besides you can be captured just as well by road pickets as by the Gestapo in Malmédy." So I fell for this suicidal policy and went and successfully demanded a ticket for Malmédy.

Malmédy, a large-sized town, was only a couple of kilometres from the Belgian border itself. Yet I had been warned that towns like Gerolstein, 30 kms away, were watched by the Gestapo. Fifteen minutes later I was sitting once again in an open carriage filled with peasant women. The next stop would be Malmédy — my terminus and indeed the last outpost of the true Reich as far as I was concerned.

Although when I entrained the snow had not started to fall, before Malmédy was reached it was coming down thick and fast. The effect when we descended was miraculous — everyone was too much concerned with his own misery to bother about the stranger in their midst, and even the Gestapo must have been completely fooled by all these white-camouflaged passengers. I approached the exit, well mixed in with the throng, and with my heart thumping gave up my ticket. Really before I knew it I was outside the station, still a free man. The smell from a baker's brought home the fact that I had eaten nothing except two

Horlicks tablets in over two days of the intense cold. In less than five minutes I was covered from head to foot with huge snowflakes. Obviously I couldn't remain walking round the town as a human snowman, yet I was afraid to leave it lest I ran foul of the Boche. The neighbouring hills seemed to frown upon me and I was sure they all harboured observation posts.

To the right suddenly appeared a little drive, covered in snow but running between two hedges. A quick look round, no one in sight, so up this lane I bolted, floundering almost knee-deep in light snow. Up and up the slope I clambered, the track getting narrower and narrower until it became a little path between high-fenced allotments. The fences screened me from view and the only risk of discovery was if a gardener chose to use the path. By the virgin state of the snow this appeared unlikely. Here I resolved to stay.

On the lee side of one of the fences I scooped out a hole large enough for my body and then crept into it and covered the lower half of my body with snow. The rest of me was quite white by this time, so unless a child happened to pass nearby I was reasonably well camouflaged. In this position, with scarcely a move, I stayed for something like seven hours. By the time it had stopped snowing an almost full moon cast a good but dispersed light through the clouds. That afternoon was, I think, the greatest trial of my life. To lie in the snow, with scarcely a movement and watch the hands of one's wristwatch creep round so slowly was more than enough to drive one mad. Inside my clothes I endeavoured to contract my body into the shortest possible space, flexing and unflexing my muscles as often as I could to ward off cramp, stimulate circulation and prevent frostbite. For the most part I talked softly to myself or kept calling on God to help me in this last hour of need. In my more lucid moments I tried to memorise my local geography, note the westing of the sun and plan my last cross-country.

At first it all seemed so simple. I had noticed on the map at Weismes that a railway ran from Malmédy to Stavelot. Obviously I had only to skirt the woods and hills to the north of Malmédy and then go south to join the track west of Malmédy, then strike a course parallel to the railway until I hit Stavelot, where I was determined to seek help. At 7 pm I roused myself and tried to stand erect. I couldn't, for the pain in my legs was excruciating. From the tip of my toes to my thighs I had pins and needles. I had to sit down and slap and massage them in an effort to reintroduce life. Gradually it did return and I was able to hobble a few painful steps. But I had to rest again and this time I used the occasion to eat half my rations — a few Horlicks tablets and a quarter-pound block of Cadbury's chocolate. At last, under cover of darkness, I crept from my hiding place and made for the wooded hills.

Down in the valley a few lights still twinkled. Near at hand some hounds began baying. Surely the frontier was not going to he guarded by dogs? I edged further up the hillside, as far as possible from civilisation and its dogs. Soon I was in the forest and busily engaged tracing a course along the numerous paths which weaved in and out. I knew it was quite wrong to follow a main path, but I hadn't the strength to go cross-country, so I chose the weakest line of resistance. Towards 10 pm I lost all track of my wanderings and most of the night was a complete nightmare.

At last I came down to the valley and the main road. Away to my right I noticed a bridge which I decided it would be unwise to cross. To my left the main road, I felt, would take me back to Malmédy. In the distance a cyclist's lamp suddenly appeared. Like a flash I crossed the road, scrambled over a sort of five-barred fence and vanished into the wood. The cyclist rode past and I pushed on into the wood which seemed to be of the orna-mental type with regular paths, and I came to the regretful conclusion that I was trespassing on someone's estate. Soon I was pulled up by the river which seemed to wind round and encompass me. Defeated by the river, the estate, the cultivated groups of trees and the regular paths, I was forced to retire to the road and instead of risking the bridge-crossing turned the other way.

As I continued along the road, glancing anxiously at my watch which now showed ten past eleven and possibly curfew, my worst fears were confirmed. I was being led back to the industrial part of the town. As there was no alternative, I went on, took a turn off the main road to the right and was rewarded by emerging from the factory sites out into the open country but still with no sign of the railway. I fished out my little swinger compass, tried to control it with my frozen fingers and then read north by the two luminous dots. Once the thing slipped from my numbed fingers and I had an anxious five minutes trying to hunt the needle in the snow. My luck held and I recovered it. So, on a good westerly bearing, I set off boldly across the fields.

Once again I met up with my old enemy, a river. It was a rushing stream, some ten to fifteen feet in width, which had not frozen completely and looked depressingly deep. Frantically I tore up and down the bank until I found a spot where the gurgle of the water announced its shallowness, and I thought I could distinguish in the rapidly rushing river some stones over which I might be able to splash. I thought of removing some clothes, but my trousers, socks and shoes were an icy mass, quite impossible to untie with my frozen fingers.

Down the bank, after a quickly murmured prayer, I crept onto the first stone, onto the second and almost into the middle, then there were no more stones. I took the next step and was plunged into the swirling stream up to my knees. As I scrambled towards the farther bank I sank lower and lower, to my hips, and then thank God, the worst had been overcome and I was scrambling out on the far side. The first contact with the water had not been such a shock as I anticipated. Compared with the coldness of the bitter winds it appeared almost warm, but when I emerged again into the wind my lower half started freezing rapidly and I gradually became a human icicle.

Before me was a long, steep, wooded slope. It took all my strength to climb it. After some two or three hundred feet I was again more or less on the level and in a very dense forest. One of the main paths went off in a westerly direction and this I followed for the next 30 minutes when lo and behold a light flickered in the distance. Help, I thought — and thanked my Deliverer.

It had stopped snowing and the light was visible over quite a distance. I approached to within a hundred yards when once again my guardian angel spoke. All I know is that a little voice whispered in my ear, "Detour. Do not proceed!" And, obedient to that voice, I relinquished all hope of food, warmth and bed and followed a path away from that magnetic light. Later I was to bless that voice, for in answer to my questions on the subject I was informed by the locals, "Oh, yes! That would be the German frontier post, there's always a light showing there!" I missed it by only a hundred yards!

It was now 3 am on Sunday, 25th January — my fourth morning out. And although I had eaten some chocolate and Horlicks I had had absolutely nothing to drink except handfuls of snow. This I sucked in large quantities without any ill effects, but now, after the night's strenuous exertions, I was really thirsty. So when I saw a quiet-looking farmhouse with a pump in the yard, I gave up all caution and tried to pump out a mouthful of water. To my surprise the pump was not frozen. I thrust my head under the tap and succeeded in not only slaking my thirst, but wetting the only remaining dry part of my top clothing. But the water did me the world of good and as my little voice still urged me on until I had definite proof I was over the frontier, I reconnoitred the farm and found a lane leading down to a minor road. In spite of the increased risk I was glad to be on the easy-going road.

Again I headed west. An hour passed by. A village began to appear. And one of the first buildings was a church. So this was it. If only I could get into the church it would be easy to prove whether it was Belgian or otherwise. Stumbling, I ran to the entrance and tried the main door. It was locked. As I stepped back to reconsider, my eye caught sight of a notice pinned to the door. Feverishly I read it. The heading was "Avis" and every word of the remainder was in French — not a trace of the dreaded German. On a sudden impulse of gratitude I kissed that notice and grasping the handle of the door I uttered a very sincere prayer of thanks. In many ways, standing there on the church threshold, I must have resembled my fleeing ancestors when they grasped the sanctuary knocker which, for them, spelt freedom, deliverance, salvation.

There were more anxious days and nights ahead, but at last I came into the safe-keeping of the gallant Belgian underground. And in Brussels, Captain Jean Sabier, a secret agent, told me of the Lizzie boys. I at once took a vow that I would join this force, which was the slender link between Britain and my Belgian friends. But I soon found that getting into this secret unit of the RAF was almost as tough a job as getting out of Germany.

Chapter 2

Captain Jean Sabier had been parachuted into Belgium from a Whitley four months before I arrived in Brussels on the Belgian underground route. He was a brave and generous man, but unfortunately he was lacking in experience. Only a fortnight after I met him he was captured by the Gestapo.

But in the meanwhile he had contacted London about me over the radio and had also been sufficiently indiscreet to tell me about a special course he had taken in England. He amazed me by drawing a small diagram illustrating four lamps and explained that on such a flare-path he could land a Lysander and have me picked up. As he attempted to describe a jet-black Lysander with a long, cylindrical tank like a torpedo hanging from the fuselage, I began to see daylight. In 1941, I had spent some six months down at Tangmere, near Chichester, Sussex, and there on the station, set well apart from our warlike Spitfires, were two shining black Lysanders with these hideous encumbrances. Naturally our curiosity was aroused but we were easily satisfied by the explanation that they did photographic reconnaissance by night, using special flash flares. Once, on the same aerodrome, when a Whitley crashed at night and five civilian bodies were fished out from the wreckage in addition to the crew, we accepted the story that they were the more daring of our press reporters, who had been watching a raid. We did not know that they were a group of parachute agents who had been prevented from jumping by the weather.

After Jean's capture and the breaking of the link with England, I spoke with several members of the underground about the air courier. Fields were inspected and signalling directions and flare-paths planned — all was ready for my return. Then I found a passage to Gibraltar had been organised, and it was there

I made a very lucky encounter. In May 1942, Lieutenant James Langley of MI9 was on a duty visit to Gibraltar, and it was to him that I reported. After a long interview he asked me what I expected to do in the future. With great excitement I told him of my scheme: the opening of an air-taxi service to occupied Belgium. "Splendid" he said. "You are just the man we are looking for."

Apparently the scheme Jean had spoken of was only in its infancy, and pilots, preferably with experience of Resistance work and conscious of their debt to their Continental allies, were badly needed. But, because of the secrecy it was impossible to make a public call for volunteers. Unfortunately, I had few of the qualifications demanded. I was not commissioned, my French was not fluent, nor had I 1,000 flying hours and, much more important, 500 by night.

Worse still, the Air Ministry clamped down and said that no prisoner of war would participate in further operational flying in the same theatre. North Africa or nothing, as they put it. In view of these obstacles, it was entirely due to the untiring efforts of Jimmy Langley that eventually I did become a Lysander boy. I believe he was more pleased than I was when my first "op" turned out to be successful. I would have hated letting Jimmy down.

One day in June 1942 I received a postagram requesting my presence at an interview with Wing Commander Fielden, CO of 161 Squadron, at Tempsford. I flew into the station on the morning of that day only to find everything surprisingly quiet and the W/C still in bed. All I could make out was that "Ops were on last night". Just before lunch, when I was in despair, I was told that the CO was ready to receive me. I went in and was immediately struck by the charm of the Captain of the King's Flight, "Mouse" Fielden, resplendent in his red braces and red-lined tunic. Then, as ever after, he was exceedingly pleasant and patient with me, and I soon guessed that Jimmy must have put in a lot of ground work.

In spite of my lack of qualifications he conceded that, given a prolonged period of special training and, more important, the correct psychological adaptation, I might conceivably make the grade. The "Mouse" impressed upon me the fact that the job was purely voluntary — at any time, if I wished to withdraw, all that was necessary was to say the word. On such a flight as this there was room only for the keenest of the keen. Without hesitation I accepted, and promised to return as soon as the lecture tour on which I was engaged had been completed. Now that I had accepted and vowed myself to secrecy, the more technical side of the job had to be explained by my future flight commander, who was already waiting in another office.

As I entered the rather dark, untidy flight dispersal littered with lockers, I was confronted by the curious gaze of four pairs of eyes — one of which commanded my immediate attention. Sitting at ease behind the one desk in the room was, I thought, the modern equivalent of Lucifer. That was my first impression of Guy Lockhart, as I took in the rank of squadron leader, the DFC and the French wings worn on the left pocket. I realised that this was to be my superior officer for many months to come. And during those months I was never to change my opinion as to his satanic influence. I respected him, admired him, and was fascinated by his personality, but all the time I was terrified by him. In the first moments of that meeting, an invisible barrier sprung up between us and remained.

He addressed me curtly, but with a pleasant-sounding voice, and after gleaning a little of my previous history, helped to put me at ease by explaining that he too had been shot down in a Spitfire the day after I had fallen. His parachute had failed to open completely, with the result that he had gone crashing to earth with broken ribs and legs. By crawling and dragging himself over the ground he managed to gain the safety of a French farmhouse, and an eventual route of escape to England. After that, fired with thoughts of gratitude, he had gone into the Lysander racket and in eight months had rocketed from sergeant pilot to squadron leader.

Up to this time I had been told stories of the glamour and heroics of this little band — now Guy was to attempt to shatter my illusions completely. In fact, he did everything to dissuade me from volunteering. Briefly he outlined the history: how in 1940, soon after Dunkirk, a pilot went out to seek a lonely spot in France where he would find friends waiting; that first man never returned nor was any news ever received of his fate. Next, after three months' practice in this country an RAF chap was para-chuted in near his own home in France and later, thanks to the previous intensive training, the pilot, F/L Farley, made a perfect landing and picked him up.

Then, however, the trouble started. The radio went out of action, clouds covered the return journey and after a nine-hour trip, completely lost and without more fuel, the pilot crash-landed, not knowing whether he was in Northern Ireland or Norway. After several false alarms occasioned by the local dialect, they found that they were in Oban in Scotland, some 600 miles north of the home base.

Gordon Scotter and John Nesbitt-Dufort came, did three or four operations and went on to other things. Another young pilot came along and vanished on his first flight; later he turned up in a French prison near Nice. Immediately before Guy, Sticky Murphy had been CO of the Lysander flight, did four Lysander pick-ups and then returned to the more routine air force. I well remember Guy's words: "There have been up to the present thirteen or fourteen successful operations — so far no one has lasted for more than five. My fifth last month."

"So much for the casualty side," Guy went on. "There is the

mental stress to consider. Ops are on, ops are off, Air Ministry can never tell you until the very last minute, so much depends on the final wireless signal from the operator in France. Sometimes you are actually strapped in the plane before news of cancellation comes through. Worse still, it sometimes happens that the message is not decoded in time, and you spend hours stuffed in a turbulent, obstinate aircraft, peering out in the darkness, trying by the light of the moon, if you are lucky enough to fly on a cloudless night, to map-read your way hundreds of miles into France, searching for some miserable plot of land which from the air looks no bigger than a pocket handkerchief. No. It is not a pleasant job, and I would not recommend anyone to try it. Do not be deceived by the glamour."

These last words set light to the antagonism already smouldering within me and, more in defiance than anything else I replied, "If you will have me, I would rather like a try." Guy shrugged. He had done his best — my blood was on my own hands.

One month later I reported for duty. Major Tony Bertram, in charge of training future operators, explained to me exactly what was expected of me in this life with the members of the Resistance. First of all, a fortnight a month was devoted to the training of agents, one of whose jobs after being parachuted in, was to find and send descriptions of any likely landing grounds in France. Roughly speaking, they had to find grassland, reasonably level and free from stones and slopes, which would give approximately 600 metres in all directions, or at least into that of the prevailing wind. Our light, parasol-winged monoplanes did not like being landed cross-wind. Once the field was located they had to send a coded description of it by radio, which was not at all an easy matter.

At this end, we then had to locate it on a large-scale map and request that a Spitfire of the Photographic Reconnaissance Unit be sent out to photograph the area from a height of 28,000 feet. This photo in turn was handed over to the photo interpreters who attempted to tie it up with the description in hand. More often than not there used to be considerable discrepancies in making an adequate survey of the field. In the midst of German-held France one could not very well stride round the fields in quite the same manner as we practised in England — even over here our surveying antics brought enquiries from curious farmers.

Thus the training was roughly divided into two halves: first of all the finding of fields, which were all too scarce in our neighbourhood, and the reporting upon them in a coded form; secondly, the actual laying of flare-paths, with particular reference to the wind and obstacles likely to upset the pilot in his approach and take-off. The flare-path consisted merely of three hand-torches which we christened lamps A and B and C laid out so as to form an inverted L, the base being 50 metres and the length 150 metres.

The operator was expected to stand by light A and, on hearing the aircraft overhead, signal the challenge letter agreed. The aircraft on seeing this would flash out a letter of reply, whereupon the operator would light lamp A, while an assistant would light C, run to B, light it and stand well to the left of the line A-B. As soon as possible the aircraft would approach into the wind, land on the right of A, run in between B and C, eventually pull up and taxi back to A, where the pilot would throttle back and wait while agents disembarked and the courier and more passengers would be stowed aboard.

At first sight it would appear that a field of 600 metres was much too large — Lysanders when practising only use 150-200 yards at the most. However, when we consider that an operational Lysander was carrying almost an extra ton in weight, that the pilot was exhausted by his long, arduous flight, that he had never set eyes on the field before, and that frequently the weather was very poor indeed, there was a little excuse for not asking for a few additional yards of security. More often than not it was quite unnecessary, but there were occasions when those yards spelt success instead of disaster.

Before I could start training with the Joes, as our agent-students were familiarly called, I was given a familiarisation trip in a Lysander. I did not like my initial flight. After the delicate handling of a Spitfire, the Lizzie with its stiff controls reminded me more of a bomber. And as I dropped the speed before landing, the automatic slats and interlinked flaps burst out with a mighty rush, most terrifying to the novice. Many passengers returning to England have told me that at the moment of landing they thought they were going to be plunged to death after the supposed snapping and breaking-up of a wing.

Once this initial trip was completed, it was my daily task to fly over to our small practice field at Somersham, where I would find Major Bertram and six students waiting for me with a flare-path prepared with yellow pickets for daylight use. Each pupil in turn would become chief of an operation: he would signal to me, I would waggle my wings and then he would stick up the pickets and I would endeavour to land, taxi back, and have the luggage and passengers changed before a fresh take-off. I often wonder who was the most terrified at the time: the Joe in the back of the Lysander, the Joes watching, or myself.

For in the first stages I found a combination of strange aircraft, a running conversation over the intercom with my passenger, the sighting of those ridiculously small pickets, and the landing within ten yards of A too much for me. My original landings were more arrivals than anything else. It is an ever-lasting tribute to the sturdiness of the Lysander's undercarriage that not one fractured during my initial training.

In time I became more accustomed to the eccentricities of the Lysander, where all controls appeared almost the reverse of a normal aircraft, due largely to the working of the automatic slats which gave the Lysander the most alarming rate of descent in the stall without the possibility of an incipient spin. In fact, after several sessions of twenty landings per afternoon, I began to take it as a matter of course and could even keep up a lively conversation with my Joe and inform him on the points of interest or the errors made by him or those now engaged on the operation.

Unfortunately for me, before I reached this latter stage of proficiency, I had to be introduced to the terrors of night training. I am no lover of night flying — and, after considerable experience at night, I still maintain that the old maxim holds good: "Birds and fools fly by day, but only bats and bloody fools by night."

I well remember my first experience on the improvised flare-path at Somersham. I had come over the ground early in order to attempt a few landings in the dusk, but because of unforeseen hitches my first take-off had to be delayed until it was quite dark. As I took off the lamps were extinguished and I was supposed to fly away and then return to the field, receive and acknowledge the signal, whereupon the flare-path would be lit and I would come in and land. In a very uncertain and shaky manner I managed to pull off a couple of landings and then, as it became really pitch dark, I leapt into the air for the third try. I flew away and tried to navigate back to the field. I assumed I was overhead, but no signal came up from the ground. Suddenly I was seized with panic and realised I had lost the field. What a complete fool I felt! In desperation I flew round in circles, vainly chasing every light I could see: motor cars on the road, cyclists with their bobbing lights, houses with poor blackout.

Just when I had given up hope and was preparing to call the aerodrome for a homing by radio, I observed the familiar dash, dot, dot come up from below. Frantically I Morsed the letter "W" back and to my relief first lamp A was lit and then as I circled, C and B came on in turn. Rather like a bull in a china shop, I made one terrific rush at the flare-path, only to miss it completely and do an overshoot.   By this time I was in a complete flap and decided to put the aircraft down on my next run.   In I came screaming once again, all the demons of the hellish blackness pursuing me, gremlins pushing up my airspeed and twisting the aircraft all over the sky.   My only recollection is lamp A suddenly coming up out of the velvety blackness and a host of white, terrified faces scattering from the first picket as I landed smartly over the top with my wheel brushing those who had not time to escape.   I hit the ground with a crash and went tearing on and on and on, wondering when the opposite hedge would stop me.   At last, by vigorous application of the brakes, I pulled up and endeavoured to locate my position in the field.   It was so black that I could not even see the landing strip, so, more or less on instruments, I taxied back until I saw light A and to the waiting pupils all I could say was, "That will be enough for tonight."

Chapter 3

"No man has done more than five," Guy Lockhart had said when he told me of the dangers of the Lysander racket. A few mornings after I had been posted to Tempsford, I came down to find an air of tension in the mess. Last night's Lysander had failed to return to Tangmere. It was Guy Lockhart's sixth operation.

But thirteen days later, a Whitley flew into Tempsford, and from it, dressed in khaki shorts and shirt, stepped a tanned and healthy-looking Guy. This was his story: he had made a perfectly normal landing on the other side, but in taxiing round lamp C one wheel had slipped into a ditch and the undercarriage was smashed. The operator had arrived on the field late and drunk. The lamps had been carelessly laid out with the result that the ditch, instead of being at the safety distance of 50 metres, was actually in the landing strip. Guy burned the Lysander, and then beat a retreat down to the south of France where he was supposed to make a rendezvous with a special-mission fishing boat from Gibraltar. The meeting was surprised by the Germans and Guy only managed to escape by ramming a German in the stomach with his head and than jumping on his face as he went down. Guy, alone of escapees, waded out and caught the retreating boat. Four days at sea, a spot of sunbathing on the Rock, and then a squadron Whitley lifted him home.

After this escape — it was the fastest evasion on record — we expected that Guy would be rested. A supernumerary S/L, Hugh Verity, was posted to the flight. Hugh was a university air squadron pilot of 1937 vintage and had a successful tour on night-fighter Beaufighters behind him. He had once force-landed in Eire, and had been interned until, in the company of five others, he made the first escape from Eire to the UK. In Fighter Command, as a night-intruder controller, he had been fascinated by the plots of the tiny Lysanders creeping across the ops board, disappearing for hours in France only to reappear at the same spot on the French coast and crawl back to base. Once he had discovered the secret of the "pick-up" Lysander he wasted no time in securing a posting. Hugh was an invaluable asset to the flight: his perfect French, his night experience, and long association with Fighter Command HQ all made for smooth running. To him more than anyone else I would say thanks were due for the bus-like service subsequently rendered by the Lysanders.

The Verity service became renowned amongst the Resistance for sure delivery. More than once, when every other command in the Royal Air Force cancelled operations for the night, the Lysanders went out to brave weather which was more deadly than the enemy. Whenever there was a sticky job to be done, Hugh was ready to take his share and set an outstanding example. He finished his tour with twenty-four Lysander and five Hudson pick-ups to his credit — the ace of pick-up pilots.

In October, 1942, the Lysander personnel were further strengthened by the posting as squadron CO of that famous RAF character Wing Commander P. C. Pickard –"F for Freddy" in the film *Target for Tonight*. With the arrival of "Pick" a new wave of optimism and ambition swept though the squadron and we all felt that we were destined to attain even bigger and better results.

And in that same month, to everyone's amazement, a very quiet little man — P/O John Bridger — pulled off two successful operations on his first two attempts. On both occasions the fields were at maximum range, involving flights of between eight and nine hours' duration. But all we could get from Bridger was that it was "a piece of cake". His methods were incredibly painstaking. He appeared to be all method, with his various gadgets, reserve stock of maps and carefully worked out flight plans. If you followed the rules of the Bridger system, he said, you just could not go wrong. After the glamour and drama of the previous flights, Bridger appeared to introduce an element of sanity and logic. I was convinced of the soundness of his work, became a firm disciple, and never ceased asking his advice on any of a hundred and one small points.

Although I was attracted by the Bridger method, I found myself becoming firm friends with another pilot, a young, impetuous flyer named Peter Vaughan-Fowler. Peter was born to fly. His father was a RAF officer and flew in the last war, his brother, after becoming a Cranwell overall sports champion, had been killed in an aircraft in 1932, and one could see that Peter took to the air like a duck to water. His first ops were rather erratic. He missed the first trip, won on the next, lost on the third and was lucky on the following. Then he settled down and produced the most brilliant flying and the best results that we could wish for. No field was too difficult, no target too far, and weather never defeated him.

These were the personalities of the Lysander flight as I zealously tried to complete my training and so be prepared for an operation before the close of 1942. My chance came sooner than I had expected, for one day in the November moon, while all the other boys were down at Tangmere, I was called into Pick's office at Tempsford and told the details of Operation Claudine. This called for a pick-up operation in the Châteauroux area, and it was essential to take from there three passengers.

Now at that time it was a rule that only two passengers should be carried in the back of the Lysander where normally the rear gunner would sit nursing his Vickers gas-operated gun. The gun had been removed to make way for a small box-seat for two and to give additional luggage space. We could take an extra 600 lbs of luggage: general supplies for the agents and in particular delicate radio apparatus which did not survive parachuting. Our bomb spats and front-firing Brownings had also been removed to lighten the machine's weight so that on all missions we were completely unarmed except for a .38 revolver strapped to our waists.

To pick up the three agents from the field, Pick was sending two Lysanders. In the first Bridger would be the pilot, and the second would be piloted by Pick himself after little more than month's practice. If he did not arrive Bridger was to try to take all three in his rear cockpit. I protested that it was my turn to become operational. Pick was adamant he was piloting this operation, but he suggested that I should fly in the back as his passenger and help with the navigation.

So Pick and I piled into his Lysander that afternoon and flew down to our Tangmere Cottage. This aerodrome near the Sussex coast was our striking base and here the intelligence service placed a picturesque cottage at our disposal. We were not officially allowed to use the Tangmere mess and mingle with the fighter boys, lest over a noggin of beer we were pumped too much and the odd secret allowed to slip. Instead, the six of us were luxuriously installed in splendid isolation in the cottage, well looked after by two flight sergeants provided by the Deputy Assistant Provost Marshal at Group HQ and mothered by the area security officer supplied especially for the job by the Air Ministry.

Cottage life ran smoothly. We would breakfast about 10 am, proceed to do air tests on our individual aircraft and then, if ops were on, the fun would really start. A scrambler telephone was linked to the Air Ministry so that any secret information could be discussed outright. The afternoon was spent on telephone calls, map-cutting, the study of photographs, flight plans, and, most important, the almost hourly consideration of the meteorological information. In our efforts to get the best possible gen, besides using our own forecaster, we would ring Group and Fighter Command and the Photographic Reconnaissance Unit; often information from daylight intruder operations could give us the required line. Towards evening the tension would increase. Just before dinner, staff cars would arrive from London bringing members of the intelligence service as escorts to the passengers-to-be, briefcases full of last-minute information and signals from the agents on the other side.

Some groups of operators were so well organised that they had radio transmitters within ten miles of the field and could send a last-minute message giving details of local weather and general security. News of that kind was unfortunately rare, but when it did arrive it was most reassuring to the pilot. One was always pleased to know that the operator was on the spot and ready to receive. So many times, because of Gestapo intervention, the Lysander made the rendezvous only to find no welcoming light as a greeting.

The Lysander service was almost a personal affair between pilot and operator or passenger. So we would meet the passengers as soon as they arrived; more often than not we had already met before in the training field of Somersham, and after introductions we would all sit down and take dinner together. Dinner on an ops night was invariably quite a ceremony — rather in the nature of a Last Supper for the poor old Joe who was returning to the stricken fields of France. Certainly food, wine and spirits were there in plenty, and unless we were actually flying ourselves a good time was had by all.

On the particular day of Pick's first operation, we arrived down at Tangmere rather late in the afternoon, and as we were scheduled for an early take-off because of the moon state, I set to work at once preparing two sets of maps. Our map-making was an elaborate affair and would have caused any navigation officer or storekeeper to have a fit. Because we travelled such long distances, sometimes our track would involve using four or even five large sheets of maps. Obviously it was impractical to carry these and study them in the front cockpit of a Lysander, so we used to join all the sheets together, draw our track line, and mark off on this each 50 miles as a navigational aid. Afterwards we would mark off perhaps 50 miles on either side of the original track and cut down these lines, leaving us with a single sheet roughly twelve inches wide and perhaps thirty inches long. This would be carefully folded into five-inch sections each mounted on cardboard, making a very stiff, compact and easily accessible map. Sometimes, especially when the weather was bad, or the field difficult to find, those maps were given much hard wear — the cardboard stiffening was most necessary.

That night dinner was quite early and I remember as Pick, Bridger and I sat down with our two passengers and hosts of escorting officers, that suddenly I felt a queer emptiness in my tummy, and in spite of the excellent food before me, all appetite had vanished. After the rather unsuccessful meal, the pilots rushed upstairs to change; we were all incredibly escape-conscious and invariably took a full kit of civilian clothes with us, besides odd escape boxes, compasses, maps and knives.

First Pick and I were driven out to the Lysander which was standing in a secluded dispersal point, and checked the position of the luggage which had already been stowed away in the rear cockpit. Six hundred extra pounds of suitcases in the back of a Lizzie is quite a large load, and I always checked that it had been stowed in the most careful manner.

Mae Wests and parachutes were also provided for the passengers, who were fitted before going aboard — on the return journey it was a very clever person who could fit on a Mae West and parachute in the close confines of a Lysander. Gradually we ceased to bother with such appliances, and it became a squadron rule that no matter what happened the pilot would attempt to land the machine — in no circumstances would he bale out and leave his passengers. How carefully and at what cost that rule was observed I will tell later.

The last stage in the ritual of a Lizzie take-off was that the pilot climbed up into the cockpit, was strapped in by his ground-crew, and then his pistol, thermos, and last of all the precious maps would be handed up. When absolutely set, he would give the "All Clear" — "Contact" and start the engine. As the engine was ticking over in its warm-up, the car with the Joes would arrive and after a last hurried farewell they would be bundled in the back, the rear hood fastened and the pilot was given the OK to open the throttle. I always felt that it was this moment that was the most impressive of all — in fact a perfect picture. The black Lysander, dimly lit by the moon overhead, the ghostly pilot caught by the weak orange rays of the cockpit lights, and the belching exhausts stubs of the motor as each magneto was in turn tested at full throttle. The old Lizzie used to stand there quivering like a horse before the race, waiting for its master to give the word of command. The thought that in a few hours time the aircraft would be touching down on some little strip of land in German-held France never failed to thrill me.

We made a habit of crossing the French coast near Cabourg, just north of Caen — exactly the site chosen for the D-Day landings. It meant 110 miles of Channel to cross, usually with a headwind to contend with. As we tried to climb the Lizzie up to 6,000 feet before the French coast, our speed was never in excess of 120 mph which meant almost an hour for the Channel crossing. On that first trip, with nothing to occupy my mind, it seemed an eternity. It was a great relief to me when Pick called up saying that the French coast was in sight and could I try to pinpoint as we crossed in. The passengers in our converted Lysanders had to sit looking rearwards over the tail; a most uncomfortable position accentuating the difficulties of map-reading, and although the moon was bright in the cloudless sky, I was unable to pinpoint our place of entry.

I was much comforted by Pick saying that we were five miles to starboard of our track. Once over the country we began to lose height fairly rapidly in a gentle weaving action and soon we were down to 1,500 feet and able to study the detail of the country more thoroughly. Just as I was settling down to the trip, a flak gun near the town of Falaise suddenly opened up and, exactly like a Roman candle, a string of golden balls of fire came drifting slowly up behind us. As soon as Pick saw the tracer he took evasive action and none succeeded in scorching the aircraft.

We flew on for approximately one hour and all the time I was trying to fool myself that I knew exactly where we were when Pick calmly announced that the river Loire was in sight. Sure enough, there was the huge silver snake glistening in the reflected moonbeams, stretching for miles to left and right of us. We had decided to make a rendezvous at Blois with Bridger and as Pick turned to port and flew along the river, within less than three minutes I saw the gleaming white town of Blois with its bridge and castles, heard Pick call up on the radio to John and announce his arrival at the rendezvous, and back came John's reply that he was ready to pass on to the target, which was some forty miles farther south, near Châteauroux.

Now I felt a little happier, for as I crouched in the rear cockpit, with the map firmly clutched in one hand and the smothered rays from a hand torch as illumination, I was able to pinpoint our progress and watch excitedly for the signal light to appear. With about fifteen miles to go, Pick apparently decided he would try to fly direct to the target instead of to a nearby town and then follow the main road up to the field. This unannounced change of direction had me completely foxed. I panicked and lost all sense of direction. Unfortunately, five minutes later, I realised that the same thing had happened to Pick for, at the moment John Bridger called up over the radio to say he had found the field and was ready to land — were we OK? Pick asked me if I knew where we were and I was forced to reply that I had not a clue.

Pick started cursing softly to himself in the microphone when suddenly his oaths were turned to exclamations to delight for there, immediately below, was our three-torch flare-path, and the winking red and green lights of John's Lizzie attempting to attract our attention. Immediately Pick called to Bridger who took off, and without more delay we did a quick orbit and went in. The landing, loading and take-off were as smooth as a routine practice. As we rose, circling the field, I looked for a sign of life below. But already the torches on their pickets had been swept up, an after a careful search of the ground to obliterate any traces of the plane's landing, the gallant little band of operators faded away into the night. We flew on until the radio at Tangmere guided us in. Tangmere's drome system, with its hundreds of lights marking outer boundaries, perimeter, funnel and actual flare-path, compared with our last little strip, looked like Blackpool illuminations. Soon we were down and after the waiting crowd had congratulated Pick on his first trip, the cars whipped us round to the Cottage, where the Joes received a complete English welcome with a mixture of tea alternating with Scotch.

The celebrations went on long into the night, and none of us rose till lunch next day, when we found that our three agents and escorting staff had long ago gone to London. As I had not yet been baptised as a true Lysander pilot, I was forced to return to Tempsford with Pick and that night a New Zealand friend and I tore off to a further celebration at a local dance. It was a very good party, and we did not manage to crawl into bed until about 5 am.

Imagine my horror, then, when at 10 am the following day I was called into the W/C's office where Pick announced his intention of doing another op himself and said that I, as a final test, should fly to an old obsolete ground in the same neighbourhood and report whether or not it had been ploughed up. Although a sledgehammer was still knocking down the remains of my head, I felt pleased as I nodded my acceptance. But it really gave me a kick when Pick added that I could now stay down in the Cottage at Tangmere. That meant promotion to the gang.

Chapter 4

I flew down to the Cottage in my own newly allotted aircraft, "E" for Edward. The machine had not done an operation and was not liked by the other pilots. But, in the able hands of my fitter and rigger, Pankhurst and Prentice, it soon developed into the most reliable of the lot. At Tangmere I presented myself to Guy Lockhart, who confirmed my chance of doing a dummy run. This dress rehearsal I wanted more than anything, for I was by no means confident of my abilities to map-read my way, and the thought of losing my way with passengers on my first op was unbearable.

For the rest of the day I was able to concentrate on maps and flight planning. The Met men could promise nothing good — lots of cumulus cloud down to 1,500 feet, with poor visibility and little light below. I pulled out the file on Saline and found that Guy had landed there some four months before, but since then the operator informed us that the Gestapo had rendered it unusable. Guy told me to take a good look at the field as by his questions afterwards he would confirm whether or not I had been successful. I wondered what he expected me to find down there — something very obvious, he implied. There was a photograph of the field taken by the PRU pilots and because I could not carry it in the plane, I made a rough copy of it. The fact of writing down the chief landmarks did much to etch the description on my mind.

The field was only seventeen miles from a definite bend in the Loire, so I tried to memorise from the map what I could expect to find — so that during those last tense nine minutes I could keep my eyes open instead of looking at the map. Last of all, when the forecast winds were given, I worked out a flight plan: that is to say, I divided the 330-mile trip into a number of legs and calculated the course I must steer and the time taken at a fixed speed to make good my track. For example, I had to steer 185° for sixty-three minutes to make Cabourg, 165° for thirty-five minutes to Alençon and so on down to Saumur, where I should set course for the field.

By dinner time I was all set and except for a touch of the nerves all ready to tackle the job. That night, I felt a good deal more important, even though I was not carrying passengers, at least I was carrying out an important reconnaissance, or so I kidded myself. Pick was scheduled to take off at 10 pm and John Bridger, who had a long trip in front of him, about five minutes after, while I was to take to the air as soon as they were clear. Dead on time the other two vanished south, and with a good deal of ceremony and last-minute advice from Guy about the weather, I too was strapped in with all my gadgets and with the blessing of the crowd was on my way.

The first ten minutes were agony: I thought I knew my cockpit drill in a Lizzie sufficiently well, but I found myself checking and rechecking everything a thousand times. I had never flown an operational Lizzie with a full fuel load before at night, and it seemed more like some four-engined bomber than a single-engined monoplane. First my radio channels had to be checked and I had to announce being airborne; was I on the right fuel tanks? Where was the switch for the navigation lights? Had I accidentally knocked on my landing lights, as John Bridger did one night? For thirty minutes he flew with this glaring searchlight in front of him, not realising it, until he entered a cloud and thought he bad been picked up by a Hun searchlight.

Thousands of such ideas flitted across my mind and to complete my consternation, I looked at my compass and discovered that, as warned, I had not secured the verge ring completely and so was flying a hopelessly wrong course. I was forced to return to the coast of England, pinpoint Selsey Bill and start again. But after ten minutes of hellish anxiety, I began to settle down and concentrate on urging the poor old Lizzie to climb as fast as she could.

After some twenty minutes I managed to gain 6,000 feet and levelled out at that height. For another thirty minutes I more or less relaxed before I started peering for the outline of the French coast. Dead ahead there was a good deal of cloud, and I guessed that announced the approach of land; at the same time, in the distance, several winking beacons made their appearance, and I tried to rack my brains to estimate which was Le Havre, Cabourg, Pont de Percée, and Cherbourg.

Sitting back in the Cottage it had all seemed so simple, but now, with the mounting cloud cutting off all view of the land, I was frightened of flying in over some town and bringing on me a concentration of flak. The cloud made it impossible to pinpoint on the coast, so, much like an ostrich burying its head at the approaching storm, I dived into a cloud and, in an acute state of terror, forced on, guided by instruments only. Looking back, I think my fear of instrument flying was far greater than any I had of flak. A Lysander is not a pleasant aircraft to fly in cloud at any time, but to a comparative novice like myself it was a nightmare.

With the varying composition of the air, the engine note kept repeatedly changing — every moment I thought the end was near until we broke cloud and above me was nothing but a clear moon in a brilliant star-studded sky, while below me was a complete carpet of the whitest cloud. Not a break was there in this layer, and as I dived down and flew just over the top of it at 2,000 feet, I wondered when and where I should ever catch a glimpse of the earth again. There was no alternative but to fly on a compass course for another hour and then see, if the cloud broke, whether I could locate the Loire.

When the hour was up, the cloud still covered every inch of ground, and I fancied I must have already flown over the river.

Once or twice already I had tried to descend through the cloud, but it seemed to reach almost to the ground, certainly above the height of some of the neighbouring hills. I was just on the point of turning back when, trying to do last check of my flight plan, my spare torch failed — the original had gone long before. As it was only a contact failure, I decided to fly on and try to reassemble it in the air.

Those extra few minutes fixing my torch meant success, for suddenly the cloud began to thin and through the dispersed layers only three miles ahead of me was the long streak of silver which I felt confident was the Loire. Sure enough, as I approached I could tell by its width that it was indeed that river; but where on this river was I? I had heard tales of pilots being up to seventy miles out on their dead reckoning, so, leaving it purely to instinct, I turned to starboard and almost immediately flew over a fork in the river.

I consulted my map and could scarcely believe my eyes: after more than two hours of flying without any reference to the ground, and with no special instruments, I was no more than two miles off track. With a sigh of relief, I continued flying downstream, and soon saw the poorly blacked-out lights of Saumur, which was my main landmark. Suddenly, in my direct line, at a distance of no more than ten miles, was the brilliantly lit flarepath of a German aerodrome — was this what Guy meant? Was I to fly almost over a Hun airfield? But as the minutes passed, the lights seemed to come no nearer, and as the seven minutes crept up, one thousand feet below I could make out a small river, which farther on bounded one side of the field I was searching for. Then a white bridge crossed the river and I knew the field was below me.

I threw the Lysander round in a tight turn to port and compared the features of the field below with those of the photograph. Without doubt they were similar. With a whoop of delight I made a low-level approach and swooped over the field a couple of times at fifty feet — as far as I could make out it was still grass-covered, with no sign of ploughing. Feeling that my honour was satisfied, I regained height, made a careful note of the German airfield lighting, which still seemed the odd ten miles away, and set course for base. Once again it meant flying over cloud without sight of land, but this time it did not matter. I had achieved my object.

At the calculated time, the French coast was covered with cloud, so I had no idea when and where I left France, but I kept strictly to my compass setting until the cloud disappeared and I could make out the ripples on the moonlit sea some five thousand feet below. Once we were free of enemy territory, it was the recognised custom to call up Tangmere by radio and request a homing — at the same time our escort party could be awakened at the Cottage, and a reception for the incoming Joe laid on.

But on this particular night, I was so elated with success that I decided to continue on my course and not call up until I was on the Tangmere circuit. So without a word, on I flew until, at the estimated time there was no sign of the English coast other than the beginning of a bank of low cloud.

I tried to dive steeply to get below it, but became hopelessly entangled once again in cloud, and this time much too low to be amusing. I hurriedly called Tangmere and asked for course to steer. The answer which came back completely shattered me. I was almost in the middle of the Portsmouth balloon barrage. Operations warned me of obstacles ahead and requested a right-angled turn to seaward. It was at that moment that a huge shape came looming out of the black murk, and in an effort to evade, I all but half-rolled the Lysander, and for the next five minutes wrestled with the controls as I tried to coordinate the dozen instruments in front of me. Once I did at last manage to regain complete mastery, it was not long before Flying Control vectored me back to base. In reply to Guy's questions as to what I had found worthy of note, I proceeded to relate in infinite detail the night-flying aids on the Hun aerodrome.

As I talked I noted a smile playing around his lips, and indeed felt completely stumped when he responded rather derisively: "That was no flare-path, but the lights of a gypsy internment camp." Just then I felt rather bitter about that trick, but later I was to be thankful for that particular landmark, and also to others in France, for in their illumination of these concentration camps, the Huns provided one of the finest of night landmarks. My grief over my lack of recognition was more than compensated by the fact that at least my navigation had proved successful — for at that time I was much more concerned about a failure through bad navigation than the possibility of a disastrous landing.

Two nights later, November 21st, 1942, marked an important stage in the development of Lysander operations, and my own initiation in the racket. Air Ministry demanded four separate operations to be carried out on the same night, which was so far unheard of and taxed our resources to the full. As Guy was still officially on rest, Bridger and Peter were given two of the operations; Pick decided to attempt again a job which had failed two nights before because of local fog, and I was given the fourth, Operation Pike/Carp/Ruff, which was on a new field south of Bourges, involving a trip of about six and a half hours but presenting no major map-reading snags as it was near to a main road.

I worked out a very complicated track of approach which consisted of dodging from one major landmark to another, instead of the more conventional straight course method. I remember when Guy examined my map and calculated the extra mileage involved, he threw it away in disgust. "What is this dog-legged effort?" he asked; I said it had my complete confidence. He told me that I would never find my way to the field on such a track, and offered to take a side bet of half-a-crown on it. "And, mark you, if you miss this chance tonight, you are out!"

I never knew whether he was joking or not, but I took it seriously. Time and time again I prayed for success on that first mission. By 8 pm that night the Cottage was packed, not only with agents and escorting officers, but half the staff on the Air Ministry side, and the secret service had arrived. Strangely enough, in spite of the weird things happening to my tummy, I thoroughly enjoyed our dinner, although I reluctantly cut out drinks.

Before take-off, each pilot collected his agent and briefed him. If the passenger had not already done a Lysander course, we showed him over the rear cockpit, how to open and fasten the tricky hood, where to sit, how to don the Mae West and para- chute, where to find a thermos of coffee, and how to don the helmet and speak to the pilot. This inter-communication often caused trouble. When we talking to base, or to another aircraft, the passenger would suddenly butt in with, "What you say, pilot? I no understand" and completely jam the answer from the station called. Eventually we had to fit a cut-out switch and if the passenger did not behave, we would switch off his microphone and leave him speechless. But we preferred to be in constant communication, because as the pilot was completely blind behind to attack from the rear, it was the passenger's duty to keep his eyes open: if he spotted a German aircraft, or saw flak, or a searchlight coming up from behind, he was to press a button which flashed an emergency light in the pilot's cockpit. The pilot then immediately took evasive action. How we hated those passengers who occasionally pressed the button just for the fun of seeing what happened!

On this November night I made sure that my passenger was certain of his drill, and then we returned to the Cottage. As we had still an hour to take-off, I went up to my room, switched off the light and as I relaxed on the bed, I once again went through every detail of my flight, until I felt at last like a word-perfect actor. With thirty minutes to go, I rose and dressed — first of all thick underwear, and then, instead of a uniform, I put on complete civilian clothes, the suit that I had been given in Brussels. Many people thought that it was asking for trouble if one were caught by the Hun; but I felt that as an ex-PoW, and one in this cloak-and-dagger business, uniform would make very little difference to the Boche — if he wanted to kill you, he would.

I kept this blue Belgian suit purely as an escape outfit, and it was lined with saws, maps and compasses, while in the pockets were all the usual escape aids as well as a little fountain pen which, when used, released tear gas instead of ink. Over my civilian clothes, in order to disguise my disobedience of orders, I wore a black overall which had a number of useful pockets, and in the event of a forced landing provided excellent camouflage for night travel. On my feet I wore a pair of RAF escape boots — ordinary black fleece-lined flying boots, with a zipper front; but when the uppers were detached, one was left with a fine sturdy pair of black civilian shoes. My final accessory was a .38 revolver, strapped in a holster round my waist. One could not be certain as to who would constitute the reception party at lamp A — once there had been a German party there. It could happen again.

My dog-legged course worked like a charm, and except that I nearly flew into a marine radio mast while flying low to pinpoint a position, the whole journey, landing and return were successful.

As soon as I was twenty miles clear of France, I called up Tangmere. We used to have a little convention whereby we could announce the success or failure to the waiting crowd at the Cottage; usually base would ask us what our colour was. Sometimes an answer, red, would mean successful, and green not. On other nights the opposite would apply, so that only those with the night's code would appreciate the answer. In the excitement of the first operation I had forgotten to arrange a convention, but I felt much too happy to keep the good news to myself, so when I was asked for a homing transmission I replied; "Here is a message for my boss — he owes me half a crown."

It was a great night — each of the four pilots had been successful and Guy, as flight commander, had seen his dream come true — a host of little black aircraft carrying out a night invasion of their own. I was the happiest of men. I had begun to repay my debt to the occupied countries of Europe. I swore that I would not rest till I had lifted out of France as many people as I had known there on my escape. Strange as it may seem, that queer wish came almost exactly true.

Above: Mac McCairns (standing, second from right) and his 616 Squadron colleagues await a call to action in their ready room, 1941.

Below: Mac's crash-landed Spitfire P8500 YQ-D in a field near Gravelines. This photo and several others were taken by German soldiers as souvenirs of the incident.

Above: another view of P8500 taken by a German soldier.

Below: Mac says he was well treated by the local soldiery, receiving excellent first-aid. He is seen here being made comfortable in a staff car for his transfer to hospital.

Above: Stalag IX-C, Bad Sulza, Thuringia. The prisoners' compound is on the left, the German barracks on the right. Photo courtesy of Heinz Renkel.

Below: the Lizzie Boys. Left to right: Mac McCairns, Hugh Verity (supernumerary squadron leader), P. C. Pickard (squadron commander), Peter Vaughan-Fowler, Bunny Rymills.

Above: Tangmere Cottage, home-from-home for the Lizzie Boys and the operations centre for the Special Duties flights. The Cottage was located just outside the gates of RAF Tangmere for privacy, and had its own security and catering arrangements.

Below: the Cottage had its own permanent staff, responsible directly to the Air Ministry, headed by Squadron Leader John Hunt (seated, centre), a celebrated pianist in civilian life.

Above: the reception room, Tangmere Cottage.

Below: Mac with his fitter and rigger, Pankhurst and Prentice.

Above: Mac and "E" for Edward, V9822, with its newly painted mascot, Popeye.

Below: Hugh Verity (arms crossed) is pictured with (left to right) Robin Hooper, Mac McCairns, Peter Vaughan-Fowler, Bunny Rymills, and Stephen Hankey.

Above: Popeye with 25 stars, the last earned on 17 November 1943, the day Mac's tour of duty as a pilot with 161 Squadron came to an end.

Below: as an Air Ministry Special Duties instructor, Mac demonstrates landing field set-up on a sand table to a group of operators under training at Brindisi.

Above: the improvised dispersal at Brindisi.

Below: Mac (on the left) with Raoul Berry and Peter Vaughan-Fowler at Brindisi.

Chapter 5

Two days after my Lizzie, "E" for Edward, had won her first star, an operation was mounted which required the lifting of two men, a woman and two children — one of the passengers being an ace French secret agent. It was decided to attempt the operation with two Lysanders, and Peter Vaughan-Fowler and I were chosen for the job. Fortunately it was not a long trip; the field was twenty miles to the east of Les Andelys on the Seine but to be on the safe side we routed ourselves in via Cabourg and then decided to fly more or less parallel to the coast until we reached the Seine.

The Service this side considered it imperative that both should land or neither; we were not to land independently. Guy arranged a complete timetable of events for us — giving the hour for every pinpoint and a zero hour for landing — if we had not found the field by such a time we were not to land but to return to base. Peter, as senior, was to land first.

This team arrangement did not please me at all: it was not the lone-wolf type of work I had bargained for, and after our communal dinner, we were briefed by different people, all with varying ideas. Some seemed to suggest we should act independently, while Air Ministry itself stated that the operation must be done as a whole. In rather a haze when the time of take-off was near, I rode out to the plane, and with an apprehensive look at the thick, low clouds, climbed into my plane and went through all the usual drill.

By keeping radio contact with each other, Peter and I managed to taxi in the pitch blackness to the flare-path and then take off together. At first I followed his navigation lights, and as we crossed out from the English coast, he extinguished them, leaving only two minute blue lamps. We were forced to fly at a height of 500 feet. In the gathering mists I had to cling close to

Peter to avoid losing sight of the two wretched little lights, which I tried to follow as they seemed to dance up and down. After about forty minutes of this torture, my eyes were popping out of head and I felt that I should spin in at any moment.

For another ten minutes I kept it up. Then the lights disappeared and I heard Peter's voice over the R/T: "Keep dead ahead for the coast", so immediately I transferred my attention to the instruments. Eventually I discovered myself some twenty miles to the south of Les Andelys, and as I flew up and down the river, Peter called up to say he was at our rendezvous point, 300 feet over the bridge at Les Andelys.

Five minutes later I too verified the position and asked Peter to proceed to target; I would follow in two minutes. The field was well chosen, on the eastern tip of the Bois de Lyons, and as I flew the twenty miles to it, I was able to check my course all the time. I saw the letter B for Beer flash from the ground exactly where I had anticipated, but this time I could not reply until Peter had landed. I checked over the radio and found that Peter had not seen the signal and was returning to Les Andelys for another run. I decided to return myself and if possible lead Peter in formation to the spot. But when I set course again for the field from Les Andelys, I completely missed the target. That error disturbed my calm and I went madly haring after any possible light until I had succeeded in losing myself utterly.

In the meantime, I gathered that Peter was having no better luck, when suddenly there was a complete R/T silence, and I heard no more. After thirty more minutes spent chasing round, as it was well past the zero hour, I reluctantly set course for base. Ten minutes later I heard a feeble message from Peter over the radio, but could not decipher it. Then I heard him say: "Mac. Peter. Just setting course for home." and I thought he must have been successful. I was disgusted at my own foolishness, but when I chanced to look down I recognised that I was directly over Les

Andelys, so in a last desperate attempt, just in case the operator had not left the field, for the third time I headed for the ground. As I approached, up came the letter B. Immediately I gave them G, and without further thought came in to land. Once again I was over-excited and as I arrived, I managed to drop the aircraft the last five feet, which accounted for the broken tail oleo the next morning. While the exchange of passengers took place, I questioned the operator about the arrival of the other plane. In the roar of the engine it was difficult to understand his French, but he seemed to indicate that the other plane had not landed. The news infuriated me; apparently I had prevented Peter from landing and then slipped in myself. In disgust, I told them to shut the hood, and off I went, taking an exceptionally long run in the soft ground. All the way back, I sat cursing and moaning to myself.

Without much trouble I found my way back to Tangmere and slapped the aircraft down on the runway, and then into dispersal. All my jubilation at a second successful operation was gone – I just hated everything. The secret service staff were quite decent about the whole thing and highly pleased with the catch I had produced, which was the No. 1 man, his wife and two lovely boys: four in a Lysander for the first time. Back in the Cottage, the whole story came out. Apparently Peter had never found the field, but had persisted in circling the area in the murky weather until, in the end, he had been compelled to give in – it was this message which I had indistinctly heard.

When I managed to calm down a little and talk to the passengers, I thought after all there was some justification for me. They were exceedingly charming, and I shall never forget how Madame presented me with some exquisite lipstick for my mother, and a little golden mascot for myself. These were my first tokens, and were dearly treasured.

But from the RAF point of view it was quite a different matter

— a breach of discipline had been committed. The following morning I was "on the mat" in front of Guy, who insisted that I had tried to pull a fast one, with flagrant contempt for orders. Guy refused to deal with the case, and I was sent before Pick, who explained in great detail the rigid discipline required in the flight, and then suspended both Peter and me from operations for an indefinite period. No punishment could have been more cruel — I would willingly have done a month as orderly officer, rather than take this reprimand.

For years I remembered that flight as my black operation, and it was not until after the war, when I lunched with the Petiot family in Paris and learnt how the very day after their escape the Gestapo had arrived to arrest them, that at last I felt my crime was justified. I was allowed to resume ops two days before Christmas, when a long trip was defeated by fog. Eight and a half hours strapped in a Lysander seat is no fun; it was some days before I finally recovered from cramp.

With the advent of 1943, W/C Pickard had a bright idea. The secret service were clamouring for more and more agents to be lifted from France, so Pick calmly announced that if an operator could find him a field one thousand metres long and mark off with five lamps a strip four hundred and fifty metres long, he would be prepared to land a twin-engined Hudson in France and pick up nine passengers per trip. His offer was accepted. An operator was trained and parachuted in, a field was found, and one night in January, in addition to our usual Lizzie run, a Hudson joined the stream to France. Everything went well and the landing was made with great success. But as he turned to taxi back, the nine-ton aircraft sank into the soft ground and stayed there.

It was necessary to switch off the engines and begin digging. Fortunately one of the more foresighted had provided spades and sacks in the plane. By this time the inhabitants in the local village had been roused by the peculiar whine of the American engines and, led by the Mayor himself, one by one, they trickled up to the field until there were well over one hundred helpers at the field. The air gunner, who was an enterprising Scot, even considered making a levy of ten francs per head as an entertainment tax.

After about an hour of digging the Hudson was able to roll again, but only into a fresh hole. Digging operations began anew. So it went on, from one bog to another, a grim fight against time: dawn was only two hours away and a lone Hudson over France in the daytime would have been easy prey. At last all was ready for the take-off, a quick parade of the crew made — some of whom had been busy making post-war dates with the French girls — passengers were loaded in, and at full throttle the Hudson lumbered past the five torches.

The soft ground impeded the speed and by the end of the run the Hudson was still sticking to the ground. With a last desperate effort, Pick hauled back the stick and like a lazy elephant the plane responded and lurched into the air. Not sufficiently, however, to miss the trees clumped ahead, and, as the plane staggered through them, their branches tore off the undercarriage fairings, eighteen inches of the starboard wing, and ripped the belly in odd places. It was a very battered Hudson which landed in broad daylight at Tangmere, with a mud-covered crew.

In the same month I was picked for a long trip, but as I crossed the French coast I heard faintly, and as if at an infinite distance, Tangmere ordering Tiger 37 and 49 to return to base. That meant Hugh Verity and I were recalled. I turned back after acknowledging the message, but no reply came from Hugh nor could I contact him with my radio. Tangmere homed me very carefully, and then warned me of adverse weather at base, but under their control I was able to land with a visibility of 300-400 yards. Within five hours a good sea-fog had set in, reducing visibility to not more than 100 yards. Then Hugh called up and was warned of conditions, but as he had not sufficient petrol to make for a distant diversion base, it was a matter of hit-or-miss at Tangmere. As he flew overhead, we were all up in Flying Control listening to the beat of his engine. Even from there not a sign of the flare-path was visible.

Hugh called up to say that from directly overhead he could see a faint reflection from the paraffin lamps burning below, and would try a landing. We heard him approach, well throttled back, dropping lower and lower as he felt for the ground, then as he realised it was impossible, with a roar he opened the throttle and went round again for another try.

I do not know whether Hugh counted his attempts or not, but I did. Twelve times he called to say he was coming in, and we stood there listening, seeing nothing, but everyone realising that he had one chance in a thousand. For the thirteenth time he called up and as the Lysander came sinking in without engine, I wondered what would happen. This time, at the usual moment for throttle open, there was no room, but instead a thudding crash was heard, the scream of torn metal as the plane hit the concrete runway. Ambulances, fire tenders and we ourselves all went charging madly out into the fog.

A dull glow suddenly appeared, but it was only a paraffin flare indicating the runway. We tore along until, suddenly, out of the gloom strode two jaunty figures — Hugh and his passenger. All we could get out of Hugh was "It was the abrupt bump which was so unpleasant. Let's go back and find my trilby hat." As we surveyed the remains of the Lizzie, Hugh explained that as he came over the runway not knowing his exact height, he held off the Lysander until it stalled and then dropped vertically some twenty to thirty feet, completely smashing the undercarriage and the extra fuel tank. The ground was saturated with petrol, but by some miracle it did not catch fire. Hugh's flair for night flying certainly saved his life and that of his passenger that night.

That month Guy Lockhart made his last Lysander flight. It was to the field where I had done on my first operation. Before take-off I warned him of the danger of the high radio mast and also the one objection to the field, the rough path. Guy found the field without trouble and went in to land, but this time the hump in the path succeeded in breaking his tail unit completely. This meant that his elevator controls could not be moved, and that although the aircraft would take off, it would continue to climb all the time. The only way to force down the nose would be to cut the engine. Before he attempted to take off Guy did his best to free the controls with a knife and managed to kick them free to a certain extent, but not enough to maintain a level keel.

He explained the position to his passenger, an old French pilot himself, who was willing to have a go. Once they had taken off, they continued to climb, although Guy used his knees to try to jam the stick forward when his arms became too tired. His knee caps were worn raw. The Lizzie went up and up, and the only way to lose height was to throttle back to the stall position and let the aircraft sink — a most unpleasant practice.

As if this were not enough, the defenceless Lysander, some-what off track over the Cherbourg peninsula, was jumped by seven night-flying Fw190s which poured a string of tracer just beside her. Fortunately friendly clouds were near and, with a 190 hot on his tail, Guy almost spun into the cloak of cloud. When he emerged from it the Hun had disappeared and Guy returned to base where he managed to land his crippled Lysander. Guy was put on rest, but although he had been missing a couple of times already, it was not enough. The next we heard was that he was on a Pathfinder Mosquito squadron and then a year later came the news that he had been killed in a Lancaster over central Germany. That was the end of a true pioneer.

In February 1943, I went out to pick up an English secret service agent who was in trouble down near Bordeaux. He reported that an operation could be mounted at the disused aero-drome near the town of Perigueux. With an excellent weather report — for a change — and no outbound passengers, I set out, I entered France at Pont de Percée, just to the east of Cherbourg peninsula and, for the first time, I saw the French coast perfectly. I went in exactly on track and stayed on it all the way to Tours, which I detoured, and right down to the target area. The moon was full, the air was clear and cloudless, and every object on the ground was perfectly visible. The whole trip was far too good to be true.

Soon I was over the prominent loop in the river and there, bounded by the river on three sides, was the little airport. I was so pleased with my find that for the first few seconds it did not dawn on me that there was no signal light. Then I realised that the reception committee had not yet arrived. Obedient to the rules I flew away for fifteen minutes to give the operator a little more time, and then I returned, carefully checking that it was the right spot.

There could be no mistake, but there was still no light. We always told operators that if possible we would wait one hour when they were late for rendezvous. After four visits to the field, spread over an hour, there was still no reply. I flew low over the ground to try to spot any movement; I could see none, only the landing T windsock and two small hangars, which bore white witness under the moon to the accuracy of my pinpoint. Disgusted with the bad luck which seemed to dog me since the night of the black operation, I returned to base and reported "No reception."

Next month, when the would-be operator was fished out from another field, I heard the explanation. The Gestapo had trailed him to the field when he had made his first inspection and, presuming that a Lysander operation would take place, they had arranged an ambush.

On the night of the operation, the English operator evaded capture, but had to lie hidden in a ditch while two hundred Germans circled the field and mounted machine guns and light flak guns. When the Lysander arrived, the operator attempted from concealment to flash me a series of dots — our danger signal — but these I had failed to notice. As I flew overhead he heard the word being passed round the waiting Huns: "Do not fire. Wait until the pilot lands." The fools never thought of signalling to me or laying out a dummy flare-path. I would have loved to have heard them gnashing their teeth when, after buzzing the field for the fourth time, I turned for home.

Chapter 6

When we flew down for the March moon we found an operation all ready for us, and as it was my turn, I prepared maps and plans ready for action. The weather was poor and I was feeling far from well. When the operation as cancelled, I was rather thankful and went to see the doctor, and was clapped in the sick bay with jaundice.

It was here that I received my first letter from a sympathetic WAAF friend; this kindly act laid the foundations of a great friendship which slowly turned to love. Moira was a Special Duties WAAF, which meant that she used to sit in the Ops Room at Tangmere, and as the little black aircraft moved out over the Channel at night, she would move a corresponding chip south-wards on the huge table in front of her, until we dived over the French coast and disappeared from the English radar plot. It was hard for Moira, and I used to marvel at her discretion; although she knew much, she did not know the full story, yet not once did she ask me a question.

When others were out on missions and Moira was on duty, I would go down to the Ops Room and watch her work at her little chips. Between us we evolved a new code of "success" messages. When we contacted England on return from a flight, the Controller would ask a question and our answer would give the clue to our success. When I knew Moira was on duty, it did not need much imagination to think up something highly personal and more often than not the Ops Room was delighted with our replies. Naturally the questions became more and more topical, as everyone joined in the fun, until, with the advent of the not-so-polite joke stage, the whole thing was stopped.

Fresh from sick leave, anxious to catch up with the score made by the others in the successful moon period of March, I was all ready for April. The personnel of the Lysander flight changed greatly a about this time — Pick, content with his success as a Lysander and Hudson pilot, decided to try heavy bombers. In his place the flight commander of the Halifax flight took over as squadron CO. His sympathies were naturally with the neglected parachuting Halifax pilots, and for the time being we ceased to be the blue-eyed boys. At the same time another Halifax king, Bunny Rymills, joined us and after a last hectic operation John Bridger left. He wanted more exciting fields to conquer. He joined Pick as a bomber boy and was shot down and made a PoW on his third trip.

John's last Lysander flight was made in mountainous country. Judging from the map contours, the field appeared to be on the edge of a precipice. The weather was poor. He was dodging up and down valleys, trying to avoid low cloud, when "Suddenly," he told us later, "there were lots and lots of pretty blue flashes." He realised that he had ploughed straight through a high tension cable. Next morning, his fitter unwound about five feet of thick copper cable which was wrapped tightly behind the propeller boss. Still, he persevered, and at last made the field, only to bump into a mound on his approach. The shock burst one of his tyres, although he did not know it until he made his landing.

We always held that it was impossible to take off on one wheel, and it was considered preferable to deflate the other and attempt a tyreless take-off. Out came John's commando knife as he tried to gash the thick rubber, but it was too tough. So, motioning the crowd to stand clear, he took careful aim with his .38 and put six bullets into the tyre. That did the trick. Ten minutes later, John was airborne. He told us that even without rubber tyres the good old Lizzie needed only an extra 50 yards' run. And to think that John left Lysanders for more exciting work!

Peter Vaughan-Fowler and I had come to be regarded as the

doubles experts, and whenever two Lysanders were needed at the same field, we were sent. One night in April, Peter and I were going out on one job, while another pilot was taking the most beautiful-looking French girl out to another spot. This pilot had left the lever of his transmitter in the ON position, and so everything he said in his plane was broadcast. Just after I had crossed into France, suddenly, loud and clear, came the words "Now, madame, we are approaching your beautiful country — isn't it lovely in the moonlight?" Back came the answer in a soft accented voice, "Yes, I think it is heavenly. What is the town over there?" And so it went on for thirty minutes, step by step the pilot pointing out all the landmarks to his passenger. I wondered what the German Y-service, which intercepted all our broadcasts, thought of this running commentary, and how annoyed they must have been at their inability to stop the flights.

Peter and I had found our field: the lights, organised by one of our best Lysander operators and an old French pilot, were switched on, and Peter went in while I circled the field, attempting to identify a sort of sandy gulf which seemed all too close to lamp A. Peter took off and I flew in, but I came down too low when I was still a few hundred yards from A. I continued to stay low, dragging the aircraft on with the nose up and full gun. Something loomed up ahead. I tried to climb, but it was too late. There was a crash and the sound of splintering and tearing was heard above the roar of the engine. The aircraft rose for a moment and then, as I throttled back, it crashed to a landing just by lamp A.

The landing run was small, and as I taxied back it was difficult to tell what was wrong. I summoned the operator and asked what the devil had happened. He explained that some fifty paces beyond A there was a small poplar — about twelve feet high — which I had completely demolished. This was in direct contravention of orders, because we were allowed a safety zone of one hundred metres behind A exactly for cases like this, when one landed short. Furious, I asked what damage was done to the aircraft, and he replied none other than the aerial which had been ripped away.

Without bothering to descend and check, which was just as well, or to enquire about the number of passengers, I took off, and the moment I was airborne I knew that something was radically wrong with the controls. The stick was shaking in my grasp and now and then there would be a violent snatch. Worse still, my oil temperature was creeping up until it was almost on the emergency figure.

I decided to climb up as high as possible and as there was a fair amount of medium cloud, I started forcing up on instruments. Ten minutes into the cloud, and the engine sputtered, coughed, spluttered again and went dead. Jazzing the throttle had no effect and I was in the predicament of having to concentrate on my instruments, try to locate the error if possible, and in addition talk to my passengers and warn them. Down we glided, still in cloud, and with no idea of what sort of ground was below. I wondered if the passengers had put on the two parachutes waiting for them in the back, so I called up and asked them. Something indistinct, like "Not enough" came back, so I asked how many they were. "Four" was the reply. I refused to believe it, "One, two, three, FOUR, you say?" "Yes."

I realised that we must try a forced landing. Three thousand feet to go, when suddenly I found out what was wrong. The hot air carburettor warmer had slipped out of position, allowing the carb to freeze up. Once this was rectified, the engine picked up and we were able to continue our uneasy trip back to base.

When I landed, I hopped out to survey the damage. The whole of the spinner, that is the centre portion of the propeller, had been stove in. There was enough wood round the exhaust ring to kindle several fires. The supplementary petrol tank was gashed and only just hanging on, and as for the most essential tail controls, the tail-plane was stuck on with only one bracket held by a single screw.

Maybe I am superstitious, but that night, just before take-off, my rigger had slipped me a miniature Popeye the Sailor as a good-bye mascot. The next day in conference with my crew, we decided to adopt Popeye as the patron saint of "E", and that afternoon, after a design had been approved, he was painted on the side complete with four successful sortie stars under him.

Later in the month, Hugh and Peter were scheduled for another double well south of the Loire, but the Met kings advised against the operation because coastal fog was rolling in. Hugh at the last moment declared that in view of the inadvisability of returning to the UK, he would leave the field and proceed direct to Gibraltar, where conditions were ideal. Unfortunately we could not provide any air maps at the last moment, but Hugh, tearing down a couple of wall maps of all Europe, handed one to Peter, declaring "We will fly on these".

In spite of this spirited offer, the Air Ministry would not play, and stated that the Lysanders must return to the UK. Ignoring all their warnings Peter and Hugh flew out. Six hours later they were both safely back in the Cottage with four new agents. Their gamble against forecast weather had come off — and they had the supreme satisfaction of knowing that they were the only two aircraft to leave the shores of England that night. Every other command, including the Halifax at Tempsford, had scrubbed operations. Radar even reported that not a single German aircraft could be seen in the mystic bowl. On such feats was the Lysander fame based. One of our more regular Joes said that he considered the ride from London to Chichester was more uncertain and infinitely more dangerous than a delivery trip to France. Knowing some of those Air Ministry drivers, I am rather inclined to agree with him.

Throughout the summer we had all worked very hard to make the Verity service as sure as the Green Line. The heaviest period was towards the end — I was called upon to fly five nights out of seven. By the time of the last operation, I was dog tired, and, as the specialist told me, fatigue had a serious effect. My ear drums were the most sensitive part of my body, and after two or three ops I would find myself almost completely deaf for twenty-four hours.

I well remember the best of those five ops. I was physically tired, the weather was considered quite impossible, but there was a chance that the target would be clear and base would remain open. The operation had been tried two nights before and no reception had turned up. Officials at this end admitted that they had no further information: it was definitely a 50-50 hope of success, even supposing we could cope with the weather. But, they assured me, it was most essential to take a certain person in and make contacts — the lives of some 5,000 were in danger. Would I care to take a chance? Of course I agreed, so once again the Fighter Command plotting table was kept awake by one tiny Lysander going out unescorted — not another aircraft took off that night.

The weather was not as bad as had been predicted. There was a certain amount of dodging round violent thunderstorms, and at each flash of lightning I instinctively flinched and heaved the Lysander over in violent evasive action. Flying low on the approach to the coast in the clouds and Stygian blackness, I was thankful for one streak of lightning which lit up the shore in front of me as if by day, and showed the estuary near Cabourg, confirming that I was dead on track. But the remainder of the journey, except for a few miserable rainstorms which made navigation impossible, was not too bad.

Even before I had started to circle the field, I saw rays of the signal lamp. I went in without further delay, noting that as I approached over the Route Nationale there was not a bordering row of trees as I had expected. I landed close to A, and before I had reached B, I was at a standstill. That seemed strange until I started to taxi, when I realised that I needed almost full engine to keep rolling on the gluey surface. Slowly and laboriously I made my way back to A and as I tried to swing the Lysander round into take-off position, I bogged, completely immobile.

Without switching off, I unstrapped my harness and jumped down, sinking into the soft clayey ground. I called to the chief and told him this sort of ground was quite impossible. He explained that a week ago it had been hard, cultivated ground, which had been harrowed quite flat and without bumps. But for the last 48 hours the rain had been persistent: hence the quagmire. I told him I considered take-off impossible. "Oh, oui. Ça va." was his only remark.

We emptied the machine. I instructed his assistants as to how I wanted them to push, and after checking that I had another 500 yards before the first fence, I picked up a ball of clay for a Tangmere exhibit and climbed back into the machine. With the French pushing on the side the kite, and myself giving full gas, we slewed the Lizzie round till it was facing B-C. The sole passenger climbed up the ladder into the rear and, at full bore, we went off.

At first the plane scarcely seemed to move, and then bit by bit we gained speed, and as we passed B we must have been doing about 20 mph instead of the required 70 plus. Gradually the needle crept up; I became nervous and switched on my landing light, ready to cut the engine before we hit the fence, when, after about 400 yards' run, "E" gave a last groan and bump, and we were airborne, happily skimming over the far boundary.

Once back at base, all I could do was to walk into the lounge looking like a bedraggled scarecrow and throw the mud ball at an Air Ministry type with the caustic comment, "Is that what we are supposed to land on?" Later, carefully checking the official Air

Ministry plot of the field, I saw it bore no relation to the one in which I had landed.

The end of October heralded my final moon period. I was to be put on rest as from November 17th, 1943, and given an Air Ministry appointment which entailed the approval or rejection of fields submitted by agents, as assistance in the training of Lysander operators. By this time, in just twelve months of special mission work, I had flown 32 sorties, and on 22 occasions I had managed to land. My last ambition was to bring my score up to a round 25 — I thought Popeye would look more complete if he had a 5-deep square of operational stars below him.

Straining to tackle the November ops which showed promise of being numerous, early in the moon I went out to find a field near Compiègne. I chose a new short route over Cayeux instead of the familiar Cabourg run. There was a considerable haze over France at the time, and visibility was very poor, and it was no surprise when I suddenly woke up to the fact that I was completely lost.

I thrashed round looking for some familiar landmark, but it was hopeless; so, gambling on one last chance, I made my way back to the west, called up Tangmere for a bearing, which gave me an approximate idea of my whereabouts, and then, as soon as I was sure of my position, went in for the second time. Success crowned my persistence and with little further difficulty I found the field even before I had seen a feeble signal coming up from one corner.

It was the rule that operators should always use as strong a lamp as possible — and use it as soon as they heard the aircraft. This weak torch, coupled with the fact that only two lights appeared on the ground, made me suspicious — at least if they were short of torches they could have used candles. One night Peter had landed on a flare-path entirely improvised by candles burning in tins and blazing newspapers. However the signal had been correct, so I flew low over the field and could observe nothing wrong. But where exactly I was to land, I did not know.

I did a last low-level dummy run and as I came to the field I switched on my landing light, a miniature searchlight contained in the wheel spats. I saw the crowd scatter from A. I came in and ran past the second light. As I taxied back, I had my .38 ready and, just before I reached A, I flashed on my landing light. It showed a harmless group of civilians.

I told the operator how badly he had conducted the reception. "Why were your lamps so poor?" I asked. He said that he did not wish to dazzle me so had put on paper covers. I could have killed him. He warned me that I must take off to the left of the second light — explaining that it represented C, and that B had failed — and he pointed out that, because I had not been sufficiently psychic in the air to appreciate this, I had landed well to the right of the prepared strip. Thank Heaven it was a large flat field. He promised that he would do better next time and I found difficulty in restraining myself from saying "There will be no next time, as far as I am concerned."

Without a thought about my passengers, I returned home and as we taxied to a stop at dispersal I was regaled with the sight of first one, then two, three, and at last four hefty American technical sergeants climbing out, bending down, kissing the ground and exclaiming:

"Christopher Columbus! We are in England!"

Chapter 7

During the autumn months of 1943, the code word Crossbow was heard a great deal, and anything connected with it received immediate priority. It referred to the rocket preparations being made by the Germans, and particularly to the concrete rocket sites on the French coast. At that time, no one really appreciated exactly what the Germans had up their sleeve, and any agent who could supply information on this subject was urgently in demand, so when I had the good fortune to be awarded a five-star Crossbow operation, I knew I was going for something big.

Air Ministry took us completely into their confidence, and explained that an operator who had been trained over eighteen months before, and who had not as yet done an operation, had what appeared an excellent field near Fécamp. It was only about twenty miles inland of the flak-covered French coast, less than five miles from the well-protected rocket sites, and three miles from the barracks of some 2,000 Huns. It would not do to lose one's way!

An RAF squadron leader, "Tommy" Yeo-Thomas GC, had been working at this site and now was in possession of sufficient details to make his withdrawal highly advantageous. My last briefing was that on no account was I to depart from the field with information only: conscious or otherwise, Yeo-Thomas was to be brought out in the back. The weather was not considered practical for such a sortie, and at 8 pm after I had been in acute suspense for hours, the wing commander cancelled the operation. After working my mind and body to such a pitch that I felt I could press on regardless of weather, I now felt so disappointed that I pleaded to be allowed to go and do a weather reconnaissance. One chance in a hundred might be enough; the base was going to remain clear all night. After some hesitation he agreed and we hurriedly remounted the operation. I must confess that it was a very nervous and shaky pilot who climbed into his plane that night. The black, cloud-covered sky looked ominous and I knew that once again my aircraft would be on her own in the night skies. At least I had the satisfaction of knowing that I had nothing to fear from German night-fighters. As we nosed our way slowly across the Channel, gradually the clouds came lower and lower, until there was only about 500 feet between the water and myself. The thought of entering the well-defended coast of the Pas de Calais at this height did not please me at all.

It was imperative to pinpoint on the coast and go in exactly on the dot — I could not afford to be even one mile out. After an hour of suspense, the sands of the French coast showed up in front, but I had no idea where I was. Praying that there were no E-boats lying off the coast, I turned sharply to port and flew parallel to the coast, waiting for signs of an estuary.

In time it revealed itself, but as there were several round this part of the coast, I flew on until I struck the next main promontory, when I knew that my first guess had been correct. I returned to the original point of entry and, with a last prayer for our safety and ultimate success, I went in over the coast defences at the ridiculous height of 500 feet. Not a gun opened up, and within ten minutes I had struck the little town which was my last landmark.

The field should be three minutes away, and in less than two minutes a powerful beam slashed the letter X. That agent definitely had the right ideas about torches — his was like a miniature searchlight. Miraculously the weather had improved in the last ten miles, and I was able to see the outlines of the field, which looked remarkably small. But once the lamps were turned on, I went down and touched at A and then, almost as soon as I had passed B, I noticed the colour of the ground ahead changed considerably. Instinct told me that this meant rough ploughed land, and I squeezed the brake lever as hard as possible — making the Lizzie almost stand up on its nose. And only just in time, for we skidded to a halt not more than five yards from the end of the grassland. I went back to the waiting reception, motioned the chief to come up and talk to me. He said, in English,

"Nice work. It was pouring with rain here thirty minutes ago. You have about three hundred yards in front of you for take-off. I am returning with you."

"Yeo-Thomas?" I asked.

"That's me" was the reply.

After take-off I was able to talk to him over the inter-communication and give a running commentary on our progress. He told me how he and the reception party had arrived with a hearse as part of a funeral procession. In any case, he added, we had nothing to fear on the field. Over fifty of the Maquis were guarding the surrounds.

It was useless to try to climb through the black, icy cloud, so, trusting to luck and map-reading as I had never done before, I managed to guide the Lysander out of France on the exact route we had used coming in with no sign of opposition. Less than an hour later, we were back at Tangmere. The weather was still quite serviceable and we landed safely, to bring to a successful conclusion the trickiest operation I had so far attempted. Yeo-Thomas's dramatic appearance was welcomed by everyone — we rejoiced far into the night, and the next day he was whipped away for an urgent interview with the Prime Minister himself.

I had sent in a damning report of an operator whose poor lights had nearly caused me to crash. His section, who were dealing mainly with evaders and PoWs, took this very much to heart and requested that we should mount another operation to bring five escapees and the chief out. He could then be given a refresher course and be sent back to continue his job. I was against working with him again, but as the moon was nearly over, it represented my last chance of attaining the twenty-five mark; so, reluctantly, I agreed to go out with Hugh on a double. Once again the weather was bad, and we scudded into France almost at deck level.

Both of us reached the vicinity of the field at the same time, but there was no sign of a signal. Eventually, after we had wasted some ten minutes searching the neighbourhood, Hugh spotted the faint glimmer of the signal torch and went in to land. As he took off again he flashed his navigation lights and, with their aid, I was able to locate the still dimly-lit flare-path. Fortunately the landing presented no difficulty, and with the erring operator in the back, I hurried home.

With twenty-five landings to my credit, my tour as a special mission pilot was over. Now I was to sit in London and come down to Tangmere only to watch others as they went out to baffle the Gestapo. For Hugh, too, it was the end; his job as flight commander of the Lysanders had fallen to Robin Hooper, who himself was out this night on a mission near Angoulême. Robin did not return, and after more than twenty-four hours of anxious waiting, a signal from the field arrived announcing that Robin was quite safe and in the operator's hands.

Apparently the field was incredibly soft towards the end of the run, and he had completely bogged his wheels. It was impossible to move by manpower alone, so the local farmer was knocked up and asked to supply a pair of oxen. These were yoked to the Lysander — but still it would not budge. Two more oxen were added, but when the team of four could not move the Lysander a single inch, it was decided to abandon the plane. The petrol tank was hacked open and fuel spilt all over: from a safe distance Robin threw a lighted taper and that was the end of his machine.

It was too late to pick him up that moon period, so Robin spent a comfortable holiday near Angoulême, living on the fat of the land, mixed with shopping expeditions to the nearest book-shops, and detailed excursions all over the countryside in search of further fields.

As soon as I arrived at the Air Ministry, my first job was to arrange Robin's evacuation. Any section with a field in that area was asked to contact their agent and check on its present security. Robin himself was confirming most of the fields, and he eventually put one up for approval which had been turned down previously by the Air Ministry. A photograph had been taken and the interpreters swore that there was a ditch-like depression across the middle of the field, in spite of the agent's protest to the contrary. When Robin vouched himself that no ditch existed, the field was sanctioned and a pick-up arranged for Robin in the next moon period.

It was during this period of waiting that I was told a horrible truth about Lysander pilots. The order was that Robin must never be allowed to be taken alive by the Gestapo. Robin and I had been hard at work for months on a filing system which gave details of scores of suggested fields and more than one hundred pick-up operations. For the safety of the whole of the Resistance organisation in France, it was essential that Robin did not receive torture at the hands of the Gestapo. Strangely enough, this was an angle which had not struck me as a pilot.

The night of December 16th saw the roles at Tangmere completely reversed — Hugh and I came dashing down from London in luxurious limousines with some of the agents, while in the Cottage there was a set of inexperienced pilots, with the exception of W/C Hodges, who was going to pick up Robin. Besides Operation Rescue, Stephen Hankey and Jim McBride, another excellent pilot but with only two trips' experience, were going to perform a double in the Châteauroux area. For Stephen it was a great occasion, because he was going to pick up a very dear friend of his, a middle-aged White Russian whom Stephen had trained, and for whom he had a great admiration. I think almost everyone "in the know" was down at the Cottage that night — everyone wanted to be there to greet Robin on his return and learn his story at first hand. We all went out to watch the three take off and then returned to the Cottage for a four-hour wait. About three hours later, the telephone jangled. I rushed for it and heard a report from a frantic Met officer:

"Base is closing in rapidly. Thick fog will be expected in one hour's time," he said.

I asked, "What about diversion bases?"

He replied, "Every base in southern England is already out of action. One might hold good in north Wales or in Yorkshire. Your present base at Tempsford is rapidly deteriorating."

Fifty minutes later the news came through that the W/C was approaching and he had been successful. An urgent message was radioed to him to make base at full speed, and we all dashed out to the dispersal. Soon we picked up the peculiar rhythm of the radial engine, but in a maximum visibility of 250 yards we could see nothing. We heard him circle, throttle back and approach the runway, lit by brilliant sodium flares. He came in only fifty feet up, skimming the treetops, but mercifully making straight for the runway. Once over the first flares, the Lizzie was throttled right back and some distance on we heard it land with a thud and the screech of rubber as the brakes were clamped on. Two minutes later we were overwhelming Robin as, looking the perfect Joe in civilian clothes, and speaking his beautiful French, he stepped from the back.

The joy of the moment was marred by the thought of the two Lysanders who could not be expected for at least another hour, and every moment the fog was thickening. Whenever I think of that night, I cannot help feeling how much more tragic it was for Stephen than for anyone else. I try to imagine the radio conversation that must have gone on between Stephen and his rescued friend. The joy of seeing each other again, the promise of a magnificent family reunion in London — for even their prospective wives were well acquainted — and, lastly, as Stephen was homed over the coasts of England, I feel sure he said to his old friend: "Just another five minutes and we shall be drinking a double Scotch together — here's to it."

But it was not to be. Hankey and McBride arrived almost simultaneously and as there was no question of diverting either, Hankey was taken over by Ford, a night-fighter base six miles away. There was visibility of about 100 yards. I shall never forget how we stood in the ghostly shroud of grey fog, listening to McBride's desperate efforts as, guided by the radio, he tried frantically to locate the runway at Tangmere.

Not a light was visible — we could see neither the flare-path nor the lights of Flying Control — all was a uniform greyish-black. After we had listened in agony to three successive tries by McBride, some one thought he heard a distant thud. We rang Flying Control, who said that their latest report was that the pilot was estimated two miles west of base, very low, and approaching for landing. Since then there had been complete silence.

At that moment Ford Flying Control rang up to say that they had lost contact with their pilot, but there were rumours of an explosion two miles north of base. Hurriedly gathering a crowd of helpers, we decided to start a search of the surrounding fields. We jumped into a V-8 staff car and with an MTC driver at the wheel, we tried to nose our way out of the aerodrome onto the main road. The fog was so thick that driving was impossible. We went off the small aerodrome road, and the next thing I knew dead ahead was a yawning hole. Down we went, half rolling at the same time. An anti-tank ditch had claimed its first victim. We extricated ourselves without injury and tore off afresh on foot, guided mainly by instinct.

For at least fifteen minutes, in a sort of frenzied delirium, I ran on, jumping ditches, scrambling over barbed-wire fences and sinking up to my ankles in ploughed fields. At last I found what I had been looking for — in the red glow ahead I saw the skeleton of a burning Lysander. Beside it was a small cluster of half-a-dozen people, impotent to do anything against the white heat of the flaming machine.

"Where is the pilot?" I called out, and a little civilian man answered, "La-bas", pointing dismally at the funeral pyre. I grabbed the little man, "You were a passenger?" "Yes, I and my wife here."

I couldn't believe it, until he explained that the machine, after crashing into some trees, had somersaulted but before the flames had taken hold he and his wife had managed to get out through the side of the Lysander. How they did it we never knew: there was no hole large enough for the human body to squeeze through; the passengers did not remember how but certainly the orthodox exit was never used, because it was buried in the ground. As soon as they were out, despite the mounting flames, man and wife both tore to the pilot's assistance and tried to lift out his unconscious body. But his legs were trapped beneath the pushed-back engine and with severely burnt hands the two gallant French had to withdraw. As the flames started licking at his body the pilot stirred, tried to move and then mercifully collapsed for the last time. For ten minutes the terrified couple had to endure this ordeal before the first of the rescue party arrived, too late to be of any assistance.

As I looked round, I noticed just on the edge of the field the green lights from a railway signal standard peeping through the fog. I often wonder whether McBride had been coming in "on the green." Meanwhile, an independent search party was scouring the fields around Ford for Hankey's plane and came upon an even worse scene. For this time there was not a single survivor — the Lysander had crashed at high speed and the impact had flung the debris over half the small field. Although it was a tremendous price to pay, the sortie had not been in vain. By some fluke the courier had been thrown clear of the fire and his body was recovered intact. Investigation proved that the information he was carrying, which dealt exclusively with the Nazi rocket preparations, was of priceless value to the nation. In fact it was a lasting memorial to the gallant pair who so nobly upheld the tradition of the Lysander pilots:

> They will never desert their passengers; under no condition will they bale out and leave passengers in an aircraft about to crash.

Chapter 8

After the deaths of Hankey and McBride, disaster after disaster seemed to overtake Tangmere Cottage. My New Zealander friend was shot down by flak while roving round northern France. An Australian on going to land overshot the field three times, and on the fourth attempt, floated across the strip, touched down just before the far hedge, which he hit violently and burst into flames; there were no survivors.

After all the years of flying over France, more or less untroubled by German night-fighters, one night a Canadian Mosquito pilot returned with the claim of one Henschel HS126, a parasol-winged monoplane, shot down some hundred miles inland in France. The same night one of our Lysander boys did not return. The film taken by the Mosquito showed that a mistake had been made. The plane was a Lysander. After D-Day the usual entry via Cabourg was barred and to continue the Resistance liaison, it was necessary to enter south of the Cherbourg peninsula. In July, Hysing Dahl's Lysander fell to Allied anti-aircraft guns over the Normandy beach-head. In August, the Lizzie flights from Tangmere had come to an end, and the story of special missions in northwest Europe was over.

In the meantime Peter and I had joined forces again, to introduce the Lysander technique to the forces of the central Mediterranean. Peter was given a high priority posting from his Mosquito squadron, and was allocated three junior officers to take out to southern Italy, together with four operational Lysanders. My part was that of the general Air Ministry stooge and chief training instructor, with the proviso that if everything was in full swing at the end of three months, I would be free for flying duties once again.

I jumped at the offer, packed my bag and, by February 7th,

1944, went off to Algiers and thence, as soon as policy was defined by the headquarters of the Mediterranean Allied Air Forces, on to Brindisi, the selected parent station. Outside Brindisi we requisitioned a couple of villas, set to work constructing a practice landing ground as no natural fields could be found for miles around, and within a month we were busy churning out six Lysander operations a week.

Unfortunately, my Air Ministry terms of reference were completely changed by local policy, and much against our will we found ourselves flying operations to Greece and Yugoslavia, which were already more or less openly served by Dakotas, instead of operating to northern Italy and southern France, as originally intended. But eventually we managed to get our own way and, in June, Peter set up a moon period camp in Corsica at Borgo Basia, and flew the first Lysander sortie to the south of France. July was even more successful and by August we had a fleet of five Lysanders over at Calvi, two of which had been supplied by the French Air Force and proudly bore the Croix de Lorraine.

During August, Corsica was in a ferment of excitement. It was surmised that this month would see the invasion of southern France. Already most of the aircraft of MAAF were concentrated on Corsica — 110 miles from the French mainland — whilst preparations were going on in the harbour of Ajaccio. We were inundated with requests for landings, mainly to take in senior officers of an age which rendered parachuting dangerous. Unluckily for the service, the weather was bad, fields were scarce, and the signal system to Calvi, by which messages had to be relayed via London or Algiers, made for delay.

With less than a week to go before invasion day, we still had seven operations to carry out, and fourteen officers who it was essential to introduce before the Day. Raoul Berry, an Air Ministry colleague of mine, had a brilliant idea. He flew off to

Algiers and arranged for a Dakota to be allocated to us. It was then arranged for a Frenchman to be dropped by parachute; this man had already been trained by us and knew the type of flare-path required by a Dakota: normally a path 1,000 metres long with lamps every 100 yards. The only snag was that there was a good deal of uncertainty about the condition of the field — two Lysander pilots who had landed on it swore that it was too short for a Lysander, let alone a Dakota. However the previous agent vowed there was a good 1,200 yards.

Standing orders for the operation stated categorically that a landing would be made. If necessary the aircraft was to be crash-landed. The agents must be delivered within the next forty-eight hours. The Dakota we were given was one used by Transport Command with their regular pilot and crew who had never before done a clandestine operation. I suggested that I should be allowed to go as technical adviser and also to do a thorough check on the ground. The idea was accepted and as the Dakota was waiting at Cecina in northern Italy, we arranged to transfer the Joes over there. As soon as the word came through that Charlie had been successfully parachuted in, the op was declared ready.

On the night of August 8th, five days before the provisional D-Day, with the greatest of difficulty we rigged out fourteen agents, one a woman, with Mae Wests and parachutes, and pushed them into the Dakota. Last of all, complete with my special "week-end case", I climbed aboard and we started up. Off we went into the murky weather, for Met had promised that the trip would be no picnic, and it was not. Close to the French coast we met torrential rain and violent thunderstorms, and had to go in without the required pinpoint being made.

As the mountains round about were some 5,000 feet high, we maintained a safety height of 6,000 feet, which brought us slap in the midst of a hectic electrical storm; blue flashes and sparks were to be seen all over the aircraft, while St Elmo's fire played all round the arc of our airscrews. I took my hat off to the South African skipper, F/O Rostron, for his bulldog determination. Estimating that we were near the target area, we dropped to 5,000 feet and I almost passed out with nervousness. Being a pilot-passenger on a bad weather trip is a torturing business: one has nothing to do but think. After ten minutes of searching in the storm, we were forced to abandon our quest and return to base, where, in anticipation of the evacuation of wounded Maquis fighters, a couple of ambulances were waiting.

The next day it poured continuously with rain and the bull-dozed earthen strip acting as a runway was completely water-logged. No aircraft was allowed to use it, and it was doubtful whether the laden Dakota would become unstuck on take-off. After a few taxiing trials, we loaded up and once again lined up for a take-off. We had a clear run of 2,000 yards, but as the Dakota lumbered along under full throttle, it showed very little sign of acceleration. Halfway down, the skipper started rocking it gently and gradually the speed crept up — by the end of the strip we were safely airborne.

On this night the coast was pinpointed, but as we reached the vicinity of the field, no signal welcomed us. We remained at a reasonable altitude because of neighbouring heights, and circled until we noticed, about five miles away, a triangle of lights and someone frantically signalling to us. We flew over the spot, but it looked much too undulating for a landing field, so, suspecting some sort of trap, we charged in again at low level and snapped on the small searchlight carried in the nose. In its white glare we saw a score of ragged civilians scattering madly. We flew back to our original spot, not realising that we had put the fear of death into a group of Maquis who were waiting for a parachute operation and who thought we were a German night-fighter gunning for them.

As we approached the field for the second time, the skipper

noticed a car tearing furiously along the mountain road, and every now and then a light flashed from it. Patiently we waited to decipher the next flash period, and there it was: C for Charlie — the code letter of the night. Our attention riveted on the car: we circled as it approached the field, pulled in at a farmhouse and then, by flying low we could make out a cluster of figures leave the farm and run to the field. First of all, on the boundary, a red lamp was laid as requested, and then, one by one, ten tiny dots appeared. The lamps were lit for the next 1,000 yards.

The line was not very straight, in fact towards the end, it curved inwards almost to a circle, but it was good enough. We tried to study the make-up of the strip. It puzzled us as there were three different coloured patches, almost as if three fields had been joined together. But we were satisfied that a landing could be made. What came after, no one really cared. With wheels and flaps down, we approached as slowly as possible — the skipper making a perfect landing just after the first light. We ran on quite smoothly until suddenly the colour of the vegetation changed and we came to an abrupt halt. The searchlight revealed that we were standing in thick vegetation, about eighteen inches high. Muttering a curse, our pilot applied full throttle to the port engine and we swung laboriously round. Using both engines at full power, we taxied back to the crowd.

I jumped down from the machine and immediately sought out the diminutive figure of Charlie, the chief.

"Hey, what the devil is the meaning of this? How much room have we?"

"1,200 yards," he said.

"1,200 Hades! What is this stuff we landed in?"

Then, as we walked along the strip, checking the surface, he explained. There was a run of 1,200 yards; but to camouflage it from the Germans, or from a chance aircraft, the constructor had planted a bed of lavender two hundred yards long after the first stretch of six hundred yards of good grassland. Then followed, after the lavender, a further four hundred yards of grassland, and then a crop of potatoes. I walked along the lavender bed — there it was, thick, springy vegetation, about two feet high. I tried to tell Charlie this was impossible, but he thought "the springiness would stop the aircraft sinking in." I felt like knocking his head off. Still, he was supposed to come back with us, so there would be plenty of time for that later, if . . .

I went back to the aircraft. The small interior lights of the fuselage had been switched on, dimly illuminating an amazing collection of humanity. They were sitting all along the side seats, on the floor; an assorted rabble if ever I saw one. Some were in uniform, blue or khaki, some in chic civilian clothes, some in rags. I asked Charlie how many they were. Thirty, in all, he told me: eight Frenchmen and the remainder evading Americans, mostly Fortress crews.

Hardly daring to think of the overall weight coupled with the poor take-off facilities, I hurried forward and went into conference with the skipper, explaining the distances and the lavender bed ahead. Rostron was a real press-on character, and despite his knowledge of the excessive load carried, he decided to attempt a take-off. With the engines developing their maximum power, he released the brakes and we shot off, bumping clumsily over the rough ground, but at least accelerating. We must have been nearly airborne when we reached the lavender; then, as though a giant hand had seized us, we wore pulled back, checked, and reduced to a standstill. In despair, all the pilot could do was to close the throttle, halt completely, and taxi back.

This time we went back to the extreme edge of the field, turning past the red boundary light but even that was not enough. Rostron ordered the load to be cut down to twenty-two passengers and reluctantly I broke the news that eight Americans had to descend. Never have I seen better discipline: without a murmur of questioning, the last eight aboard turned round and with only a casual,"Say, can you come for us tomorrow night?" jumped off and joined the waiting crowd.

We roared down the strip again, and as the five of us crowded in the control cabin anxiously watched the ground revealed in the searchlight's glare, I could feel the sweat trickling down my brow and dripping on the floor. One hundred yards ahead was the lavender: I glanced at the air speed indicator — 65, 66, 67 — we might just do it. There was a horrible lurch, the aircraft staggered as though hit, and the air speed needle dropped to 45 and continued falling, but this time the pilot was like a man possessed. He kept the motors turning at full pitch as we ploughed our way through two hundred yards of lavender.

At a speed of thirty miles per hour, we broke through and on to the firm grass beyond, immediately the speed increased, and as we gradually accelerated, we waited for the appearance of the potato crop. There it was, black in the rays of our lamp, and as it came nearer, we could feel our wheels occasionally leaving the ground. With ten yards to go, Rostron heaved back on the stick, and that good old Dakota responded. The main wheels cleared, and with our tail wheel still dragging in the potatoes in the most horrible nose-up position we became airborne.

As we circled the field, one by one the lights went out, leaving no sign at all of the previous hectic thirty minutes. Soon we were back at base, and as day came, we assembled the mob and took a photograph: a souvenir of the largest and last load out. For in three days' time, the invasion of the south coast took place, and thanks the Maquis no operation was ever more successful. Soon there followed the dramatic four hundred miles' march north, where Caen veterans joined forces with those of Marseilles. France was liberated, and the happy hunting ground for the pick-up boys was nothing but a pleasant memory.

Because my sympathies were essentially with the French and

Belgians, and I had no desire to operate with the Italians, as soon as I could I grabbed my bags, went to England and tried to organise a job on the Continent. The Second Tactical Air Force, operating in Belgium and Holland, seemed to offer what I wanted; so, not without many regrets, I left the secret ways of the cloak and dagger boys and returned to a more orthodox Royal Air Force — back to my first love, a fighter squadron.

J. A. McCairns
Lysander Operations with 161 Squadron, 1942-43

Date, Aircraft, Type	Name of Operation	Location of Field	Passengers to France	Passengers from France
25-26 Nov 42 V9822 Solo	Pike/Carp/ Ruff	800 m N of Chavannes, nr Bourges	J.F.G. Loncle	Col. Linares, Lt Vellaud
28-29 Nov 42 V9822 Double with V-Fowler	Perry	2 km N of Morgny, nr Rouen	None	Max & Mme Petit, two children
23-24 Dec 42 V9822 Solo	Ajax	E of Ussel	Fog over target. Abandoned.	
23-24 Jan 43 V9822 Solo	Miner	Périgeaux aerodrome	No signal. Airfield infiltrated by German troops. Aborted.	
26-27 Jan 43 V9822 Double + spare with Rymills, Verity. McC recalled to base.	Prawn/ Gurnard/ Whitebait	1 km NNE of Courlaoux, nr Lons-le-Saunier	Capt. H. Barosh landed by Rymills. R. Heritier + 1 other back to GB with McC.	Col. Manhès, J. Fleury
13-14 Feb 43 V9822 Double + spare with V-Fowler, Verity. Verity not required.	Porpoise/ Prawn/ Gurnard	2 km SSW of Ruffey-sur-Seille nr Lons-le-Saunier	Col. Manhès, R. Heritier	J. Moulin, Gen. Delestraint, P.-J. Kalb, Guigui
14-15 Apr 43 V9822 Double with V-Fowler	Salesman	1.5 km SSE of Pocé-sur-Cisse, nr Tours	J.R.A. Dubois, J. Frager, P. Liewer, J.C.G. Chartrand	M. Clech
15-16 Apr 43 V9723 Double with V-Fowler	Liberté/ Juliette	2 km N of Morgny, nr Rouen	J. Cavaillès, E. de la Vigerie, R. Tainturier	P. Brossolette, Yeo-Thomas, Capt. Ryan, A. Dewavrin, L. Jourdren

Date	Codename	Location		
19-20 Apr 43 V9723 Solo	Sabine	2.5 km WSW of Luzillé, nr Tours	Devisques, Canoirs	P. Sonneville, Cmdt & Mme Valois, S. Trifol
13-14 May 43 V9822 Solo	Jeanette	2.5 km WSW of Luzillé, nr Tours	Baird (SIS)?	F. Chatelin, J.-L. Chancel, Jeannette Guyot
11-12 Jun 43 V9822 Double with V-Fowler	Louisiane	2.5 km WSW of Luzillé, nr Tours	No reception	
13-14 June 43 V9822 Double with V-Fowler	Louisiane, 2nd attempt	2.5 km WSW of Luzillé, nr Tours	H. Morier, J.-L. Chancel, R. Galy, Guilcher + 1 other	A. Peretti, Capt. Nomy, J. Tayar, J. Robert, ? Cohen, + a lady
15-16 Jun 43 V9822 Double with V-Fowler	Nicolette	3 km NW of Gournay-sur-Aronde, nr Compiègne	3 unidentified agents	Mme Grenier, R. Hérisse, B. Cordier, A. Kohan, J. Ayral + 1 other
16-17 Jun 43 V9822 Double with Rymills	Teacher	3.5 km WNW of Villevêque, nr Angers	C. Skepper, Diana Rowden, Cecily Lefort, Noor Inayat Khan	Mme Pierre-Bloch, J. & F. Agazarian, ? Lejeune, J.-P. Vernant
15-16 Jul 43 V9822 Double with V-Fowler	Arrow	2 km NNE of Rivarennes, nr Tours	E. Laffon, M. Pascouet	R. Vivier, J. Sabatier, A. Van Wolput + 1 other
17-18 Jul 43 V9822 Solo	Athlète	1.5 km ENE of Azay-sur-Cher, nr Tours	No reception	
19-20 Jul 43 V9822 Solo	Athlète, 2nd attempt	1.5 km ENE of Azay-sur-Cher, nr Tours	I. Newman + 1 other	F. Antelme, W. Savy + 1 other

Date / Aircraft / Operation	Operation name	Location	Passengers	
22-23 Jul 43 V9822 Solo	Antirrhinum	6 km WNW of Fère-en-Tardenois, nr Soissons	Failed. Thick low cloud all the way.	
25-26 Jul 43 V9822 Solo	Antirrhinum, 2nd attempt	6 km WNW of Fère-en-Tardenois, nr Soissons	Also failed. Low cloud, visibility 1000 yards. Shot at over Creil.	
14-15 Aug 43 V9822 Double with V-Fowler	France	5.5 km N of Dun-sur-Auron, nr Bourges	A. Kohan, P. Montford, Germaine	F. Svagrovsky + 4 others
15-16 Aug 43 V9822 Double with Verity	Popgun	1 km SE of Sougé, nr Couture-sur-Loir	F. Closon, G. Degliame, G. Védy, J. Bingen	F. Delimal, H. Pergaud, Capt. C. Four, F. Fouquet, C. Pochard
20-21 Aug 43 V9822 Double with Hooper	Antirrhinum, 3rd attempt	6 km WNW of Fère-en-Tardenois, nr Soissons	Capt. J. Schaller, Deschamps	Duthilleul, R. Guattary, L. Philouze, G. Bourguignon
10-11 Sept 43 V9822 Double with Hooper	Californie	5.5 km N of Dun-sur-Auron, nr Bourges	Failed. Bad weather en route.	
11-12 Sept 43 V9822 Double with Hooper	Californie, 2nd attempt	5.5 km N of Dun-sur-Auron, nr Bourges	F. Svagrovsky, S. Trifol + 4 others	Capt. Le Crom-Hubert, J. Fleury, policeman Dubois + 3 others
12-13 Sept 43 V9822 Treble with V-Fowler, Verity	Battering Ram	2 km NNE of Rivarennes, nr Tours	Lt Col. Marchal, Col. Rondenay, Cdt Palaud, V. Abeille, A. Boulloche, J. Kammerer, H. d'Eyrames, J.-B. Allard	P. & F. Schmidt, G. & Mme Védy, Capt. E. Laffon, R. Houze + 2 others

16-17 Sept 43 V9822 Double with V-Fowler	Claudine	3 km NW of Gournay-sur-Aronde, nr Compiègne	S. Hessel	J. Guyot, R. Claudius, J. & Mme Tillier, Gen. P. Lejeune, Capt. G. Lecointre
18-19 Sept 43 V9822 Double with V-Fowler	Bomb	1.2 km S of Ambérac, nr Angoulème	Yeo-Thomas, P. Brossolette, A. Déglise-Fabre	E. Bornier, J. Pain, A. Mercier, A. Le Toquer
16-17 Oct 43 V9822 Solo	Marguerite	2 km WNW of Estrées-St-Denis, nr Compiègne	Col. H. Ziegler, A. Caffot	Abbé Vorage, Crouzillat, R. Gervais
17-18 Oct 43 V9822 Double with Bathgate	Cadeau	3.5 km NNE of Le Tranger, nr Châtillon-sur-Indre	J. Guyot, A. Boyer, Lt Col. Gentil, G. Defferre, C. Longetti + 1 other	H. Bernard, policemen Clouet & Foux, Traffeur, G. & F. Gane
18-19 Oct 43 V9822 Solo	Magdalen, 2nd attempt	2 km SW of Selens, nr Soissons	No reception	
20-21 Oct 43 V9822 Double with Hankey	Sword	1.2 km NW of Passy-sur-Seine	A. Schock, J. Aboulker + 2 others	M. Godet, A. Rousse, M. Juillet
7-8 Nov 43 V9822 Solo	Magdalen, 3rd attempt	2 km SW of Selens, nr Soissons	Lt G. d'Oultremont	USAAF NCO aircrew: H. Browning, J. Desrochers, E. Klein, A. Whalen
9-10 Nov 43 V9822 Solo	Nathalie	3 km NW of Gournay-sur-Aronde, nr Compiègne	Failed. Fog.	
11-12 Nov 43 V9822 Treble with Hooper, Bathgate	Oriel	3.5 km NNW of Haims, nr Châtellerault	Hooper found the ground dangerously soggy; instructed others not to land.	

15-16 Nov 43 V9822 Solo	Tommy Gun	1 km NW of Canettemont, nr Arras	R. Houze, G. Broussine	Yeo-Thomas, Mme M. Guyot, Mme C. Pichard
16-17 Nov 43 V9822 Double with Verity	Magdalen II	2 km SW of Selens, nr Soissons	L. Dumais, R. Labrosse	Cdt D. Potier, RAF/USAAF aircrew: V. Johnson, H. Maddox, F. Murray, C. Breuer, S. Chichester

Editor's Notes

Compiled from the information given in Appendix B of Hugh Verity's book, *We Landed by Moonlight: The Secret RAF Landings in France 1940-1944*, Revised 2nd Edition, Crécy Publishing Ltd, 2000; Pierre Tillet's "Tentative History of In/Exfiltrations into/from France during WWII from 1940 to 1945" accessed on the Internet at http://www.plan-sussex-1944.net; the No. 161 Squadron operations record book; and J. A. McCairns's flying log book and flight reports.

Due to wartime security restrictions, the agents' names were not recorded in the ORB or the pilots' flight reports made at the time. Hence the passenger lists given here are later reconstructions based on other evidence. Please refer to Verity and Tillet for their sources of information about the passengers on these flights.